Y0-BQW-986

SPANISH PAINTING

THIS VOLUME, EDITED BY
ANDRÉ GLOECKNER,
WAS FIRST PUBLISHED IN DECEMBER MCMXXXVII BY THE HYPERION PRESS, PARIS TEXT AND COLOUR PLATES PRINTED BY J.-E. GOOSSENS, BRUSSELS. PLATES IN PHOTOGRAVURE AND COLOUR BLOCKS ENGRAVED BY ETABLISSEMENTS JEAN MALVAUX; BINDING BY AUG. MEERSMANS, BRUSSELS.

7938-1

SPANISH PAINTING

BY

E. HARRIS

PARIS

THE HYPERION PRESS

FRENCH & EUROPEAN PUBLICATIONS INC.

610, FIFTH AVENUE — ROCKEFELLER CENTER NEW-YORK, N. Y.

SOLE AGENTS FOR U.S A. AND CANADA

THE LIBRARY
COLBY JUNIOR COLLEGE
NEW LONDON, N. H

ND
801
H3

N.38 5.98 Nat'l Sch. Bk. Ser.

16798

PRINTED IN BELGIUM

COPYRIGHT BY HYPERION 1937

Quien dice España dice todo.

SPAIN is a world apart from the rest of Europe, separated by climatic differences and isolated in time as well as in space. Bounded by water on three sides, and on the fourth cut off by the barrier of the Pyrenees, she was for three hundred years, from the VIIIth to the XIth centuries, virtually under the domination of an oriental power — that of the Moors, whose culture was not only more advanced than that of any part of Europe, but also profoundly different from any European civilization. Their last stronghold in the Peninsula, Granada, only fell to the Christians at the end of the XVth century.

During the period of Moorish domination Islamic and Christian culture vied with one another for predominance and their interaction was considerable; but whereas Christian influence on the Moors was merely transitory, lasting only as long as they remained in the Peninsula, Moorish influence on the character and culture of the Spanish people was permanent. Artistically, Moorish influence persisted longest in architecture and the industrial arts; in painting it was short-lived and confined to illuminated manuscripts. The history of Spanish painting proper can therefore be said to date from the beginning of the Christian reconquest of the Peninsula, when, through the consolidation of Christianity, Spain was brought into contact with Western European influences.

In the XIth and XIIth centuries Christian Spain was certainly in the vanguard of the Romanesque style, however much her contribution to its development may be disputed. Spanish Romanesque painting is, moreover, of unrivalled importance in providing material for the study of a style which was common to the rest of Europe but of which few examples have survived elsewhere. The richest collection of Romanesque wall-painting of all Europe exists in the Barcelona Museum, taken from churches in the region of the Pyrenees and Catalonia, where Moorish influence having been early overthrown, political development and commercial prosperity were most advanced, and contact with the rest of Europe closest. The existing wall-paintings consist for the most part of the decoration of the apse and walls of churches and are executed in fresco; the usual scheme of decoration of the apse contained the figure of the Pantocrator or the Virgin and Child, in a mandorla, surrounded by the symbols of the Evangelists, and, below, the twelve apostles. On the walls were represented scenes from the Old and New Testament. The decorations from the church of San Clemente de Tahull, which can be dated 1123, are amongst the finest examples of Romanesque wall-painting. The colour element is very strong, red and yellow, the basic colours used in Mozarabic illuminated manuscripts, predominating. The forms are defined in strong black outline, and expression is given by variety of gesture. Panel paintings, of which Spain again provides a unique abundance of material in the collections preserved in the Museums of Barcelona and Vich, consist of altar decorations and above all of altar-frontals. The earliest examples followed the general scheme of decoration of the apsidal paintings. In the centre of the *SS. Julitta and Quiricus* frontal are represented the two saints, in the manner of the Virgin and Child, and on either side, in two rows and in separate compartments, scenes from their lives. With the transition from Romanesque to Gothic architecture, increasing importance was given to the painted altar, and the simple form of the altar-frontal developed into the composite altar-piece; it no longer served a purpose as an altar-table but became a « picture » intended to stand on, or be hung over, the altar-table.

The XIIIth century brought the consolidation of the Christian kingdoms in Spain with the reconquest of Cordova, Seville, the Balearic Islands and Valencia from the Moors. The policy of Mediterranean expansion of the Aragonese kings, which produced the annexation of Sicily in 1284 and the conquest of Sardinia in 1324, provided much closer contact with Italy than heretofore, and this was reflected in the development of painting. Contact with Sienese art in particular was further provided by the close proximity of the papal court at Avignon, where Simone Martini and other Sienese artists were employed. The first echoes of Italian painting occur in Catalonia in the work of Ferrer Bassa, a contemporary of Giotto, who was employed by the King of Aragon. His only extant work is the series of the mural decorations in the Franciscan convent of Pedralbes (1345-6); these show a combination of Florentine and Sienese influences, and by a certain naïveté in the iconographic treatment.

Ferrer Bassa gave the direction to painting in Aragon during the rest of the XIVth century. Amongst his followers were the brothers Jaime and Pedro Serra, who played an important part in the development of the completely evolved type of Spanish Gothic retable. The *Virgin and Child* of the Román Vicente collection is one of the many versions of an iconographic type popularized by the brothers Serra and their workshop, a combination of the type of the « Nursing Madonna » with that of the « Virgin ot Humility »; the decorative effect of the composition is emphasized by the patterned gold of the Virgin's tunic and the characteristic conventionalized ornamentation of her mantle. A combination of French and Italian (Sienese) influences characterizes the work of Luis Borrassá, a pupil of the Serras, who worked chiefly in Barcelona at the end of the XIVth and beginning of the XVth centuries. His style persisted until the middle of the century, and is marked by a mannered elegance of form, the use of Gothic architecture and of contemporary costume, and a taste for genre which brought with it an exaggeration of gesture and of facial expression, combined with richness of colour.

The XVth century saw the rise in political importance of Valencia, which was later to become famous as a centre of fashion and luxury, and the development of a flourishing school of painting there. The introduction of a certain degree of German influence, manifested in much Valencian painting of this period, is attributed to the influence of Andrés Marzal de Sax, an artist possibly of German origin, who executed the altar of St. Thomas for the cathedral about 1400. Whatever its origin in Spain, the Northern tendency towards exaggerated realism corresponded to an inherent trait of the Spanish character and was therefore easily assimilated by Spanish artists.

The early XVth century altar-piece of St. George (Victoria and Albert Museum, London), which has been attributed though without convincing grounds to Marzal de Sax, is typical in form of the Spanish retable of the period which was characterized by the painted frame, known as a « guardapolvos » (dust-guard). In the centre panel St. George, patron saint of Valencia, is represented fighting at the side of the King of Aragon in his battle against the Moors. In the numerous surrounding compartments are represented scenes from the life of the saint, scenes of medieval torture in which the Northern realistic tendency towards distorted forms, grotesque facial expression and violent gesticulation is given full vent.

The introduction of Northern influence in Valencia at the beginning of the XVth century announces the general trend of painting in Spain in the second half of the century, when it developed through contact with Flanders, not only in Aragon, but also in Castile and Andalusia, where painting now began to flourish. Whether or not, Jan van Eyck formed part of the Burgundian embassy which in 1427 went to Valencia to ask the hand of the daughter of the King of Aragon for the Duke of Burgundy is not known, but it is at any rate very probable that he was in Portugal and the West of Spain in 1428-9. It is, however, in the East of the Peninsula that definite contact with Flanders can first be traced in the person of Luis Dalmau, probably a Valencian by birth, who in 1431 was pensioned to go to Flanders, and in 1443 commissioned to paint the altar of the *Virgin of the Councillors,* which obviously shows knowledge of the Ghent altar-piece.

Jacomart, who was court painter to the King of Aragon, worked for several years for him in Naples, where he is responsible for the propagation of the Hispano-Flemish style. He in his turn derived from his stay in Italy, and took back to Spain, some superficial elements of Italian Renaissance painting. In Catalonia Dalmau's influence did little more than introduce Flemish literal realism to the work of artists like Huguet and Vergós and had little lasting effect. In fact the latter part of the century saw the gradual decay of the school of Catalonia; Master Alfonso and Bermejo, who worked in Barcelona and whose art was far above the general standard of painting there, were both probably of Cordovan origin; they were moreover isolated figures and appear to have had no influence on their contemporaries — conclusive evidence of the internal decay of the Catalan school.

Although centres of painting in Spain from the XIIth century onwards were by no means confined to the kingdom of Aragon, development elsewhere was much retarded for political reasons, and it was only with the passing of political supremacy from Catalonia to Castile, and through contact with Flemish painting, that an indigenous school arose in Castile. Little is known of the beginnings or the sources of Flemish influence in Castile., but it was certainly much stronger and more productive there than elsewhere in Spain, and appeared fully established in the altar-piece of Jorge Inglés, painted about 1455 for the Marqués de Santillana.

The rise of the school of Castile, and the prolific production of the last quarter of the century corresponded to the centralization of the power of the crown by the union of the kingdoms of Aragon and Castile under Ferdinand and Isabella, and the beginning of a period of political and economical prosperity following a period of civil strife and economic depression. Isabella, moreover, was a great patron of the arts, and not only encouraged the production of painting at home but did much to foster it, and even to influence its direction, by employing Flemish artists at her court and by acquiring a large number of contemporary Flemish paintings; she was, indeed, the founder of the Spanish royal collection.

Painting in Spain had remained up to this time, and was to remain for many years longer, exclusively under the patronage of the church and the crown. From the beginning of the Christian reconquest the Spanish kings had, for political reasons, as well as for reasons of faith, placed themselves at the service of the Catholic church; for in order to win territory and power they had to fight in the name of Christianity against Islam. With the consolidation of the power of the monarchy, at the end of the XVth century, and the substitution of direct control which brought about the suppression of the nobles and the incorporation of all military orders, the crown became identified more and more closely with the Catholic church. Ferdinand and Isabella, the « Catholic monarchs », were the champions of Christianity, and worked not only for the political union of Spain, but also for religious unity; during their reign the Moors were finally vanquished, and the Jews expelled from the Peninsula. The Spanish artist, therefore, whether in the employ of crown or church was required to paint religious subjects only. Portraiture, which in Flanders had been encouraged by the patronage of the rich bourgeoisie, and in Italy by that of the ruling nobility, was, in the absence of these classes in Spain, virtually non-existent — except for the occasional representation of donors in religious compositions — until the rise of court portraiture towards the end of the XVIth century. Because, then, of this limitation of the requirements of painting and the single purpose which painting served, the Italian Renaissance never took root in Spain. Classical and mythological subjects, which, inspired by the revival of humanism, found favor in Italy even at the papal court, were not only inadmissible in Catholic Spain, but there were even no patrons for this genre.

Echoes of the Renaissance in so far as it touched the style of religious painting did, however, reach the Peninsula, and combined with the Flemish currents already existing. The Castilian Pedro Berruguete worked in Urbino together with Melozzo da Forlì and Justus of Ghent and on his return to Spain was employed to paint in the cathedral of Toledo and in the cathedral and the monastery of Santo Tomás at Avila. In Valencia contact with Italy was much closer than in any other part of Spain, partly because of geographical position — Naples, too, was reconquered by the Spaniards at the end of the XVth century — and because of the Valencian origin of Pope Alexander VI. Several Italian artists were working in Valencia at the close of the century, and the Pope sent a number of Italian paintings there. Italian Renaissance influence was consequently more extended in Valencia than elsewhere in Spain and coloured the production of painting there throughout the XVIth century. Rodrigo de Osuna the Elder and his son Rodrigo de Osuna the Younger, like the early italianizing Flemings introduced Italian Renaissance elements, especially as regards architectural backgrounds and details of decoration, into their more or less Flemish compositions. Fernando de Llanos and Fernando Yáñez de la Almudina actually studied in Italy under Leonardo da Vinci, and took his style back with them to Valencia. In the second quarter of the century Juan Vicente Masip, and later his son, known as Juan de Juanes, borrowed freely from Raphael and Leonardo, combining with Renaissance types of composition Flemish realistic detail and mannerist colouring. The production of the second half of the century was centred around Juan de Juanes and his followers. The Renaissance, however, remained essentially foreign to Spain, and the italianization of the school of Valencia corresponded to its decline into a second-rate provincial school.

In Andalusia, on the other hand, which was raised to a position of unrivalled commercial prosperity as a result of the colonization of America at the end of the XVth century, the stimulus to art provided by this increase in prosperity coincided with the introduction of Italian influence. In the XVth century the schools of Seville and Cordova, like the rest of Spain, developed under Flemish influence. At the beginning of the XVIth century Alejo Fernández was one of the first and most important artists to reflect the Renaissance in his serene and balanced compositions and elegant and idealized types. The influence of Italian mannerism soon appeared in Seville and was due to artists like Luis de Vargas and Pablo de Cespedes, who probably spent several years in Italy. Northern mannerism on the other hand was derived from actual contact with artists who, like the Fleming Peter de Kempener and the Dutchman Ferdinand Sturm worked in Seville for several years. Kempener was even considered by the early Spanish biographers as a representative of their own school and was known by a Spanish version of his name, Pedro Campana. The result of Northern manerist influence on local painting was the mediocre production of artists like Antonio de Alfian, Antonio Mohedano and Alonso Vázquez.

The artist who gave the most intense personal colour to mannerism was Luis de Morales who, because he so well expressed the intense religious devotion of his time, was known as « the Divine ». His most frequent subjects, the Virgin and Child, Christ carrying the cross, and the Virgin with the dead Christ, reveal by means of a combination of archaistic Gothic forms and dramatic lighting a sincerity and intensity of religious emotion — even of religious mysticism — of a highly personal and at the same time very Spanish character.

The translation of mannerism into Spanish idiom bore the germs of those essential characteristics of Spanish painting which found full expression in the XVIIth century. Navarrete, « el Mudo », who was employed in 1568 by Philip II to work in the Monastery of San Lorenzo which he had built at El Escorial, though not a painter of very high merit, is seen in a work like the *Burial of St. Lawrence* to be the forerunner of the « tenebrist » painters of the following century. Navarrete died in 1579 and Philip, having failed to attract the great Venetian painters to Spain, had to fall back on artists like

Luca Cambiaso, Federico Zuccaro and Pellegrino Tibaldi as well as the mediocre Spanish followers of Navarrete for the decoration of his monastery.

The court of Philip II was, however, more important in its influence on the direction of portrait painting than of religious painting and at it was inaugurated a style of aristocratic court portraiture which was to culminate in the portraits of Velázquez. The artist who was primarily responsible for the development of portrait painting in Spain was the Dutchman Anthonis Mor who worked at the Spanish court. Alonso Sánchez Coello succeeded Mor in his position at the court and continued his style; though his modelling is weaker and he tends towards a less strictly linear execution, he preserves the stiffness and formality of posture which reflect the severity of the conventions of court life and which the fashions in Spanish court dress enhanced. Pantoja de la Cruz, a follower of Sánchez Coello, continued this tradition, though in a more intimate portrait such as that of Fray Hernando de Roxas, his style became emancipated from the severe formula imposed by his court portraits.

In contrast to the insipid mannerism of the later generation of artists working in the Escorial, and to the strict conventionalism of the court portrait painters, the personality of one artist rose above all others to embody qualities of an essentially Spanish character in a purely personal idiom, and this artist was a foreigner by birth. El Greco, born in Crete and educated in Italy must nevertheless be considered as the first great Spanish painter, for his personality as an artist, though formed in Italy, only reached its full development in Spain. Born in 1541, El Greco was established in Toledo by 1577. In his early works there, such as the *Trinity,* he continued in the mannerist style of his Italian period, but this style soon became imbued with an increasingly personal and increasingly Spanish character, due, not to the influence of Spanish art, but to the influence of the character of the country and of the people and to the atmosphere of Spain.

The Burial of Count Orgaz is, as it were, a protest against the false pomp of mannerism. The studied concentration of composition, and sobriety of colour are miraculously suited to the subject, that of a Spanish nobleman who, because he « served God and his Saints », was rewarded by being buried by SS. Stephen and Augustine; in the portrait heads of the row of Spanish noblemen who form a background to the burial, El Greco introduces a new note of realism. Although on several occasions condemned by the church for « improprieties », El Greco was above all else a religious painter and, except for portraits, worked exclusively for the church. As he developed in style towards the baroque, he gave even fuller expression to the dogma of the Catholic church. No artist has represented more completely the visual appearance of religious ecstacy, an emotional moment in terms of line and colour. In the *Assumption of the Virgin,* painted in the year of his death, in 1614, he abandoned all formal modelling and has represented the moment in which the Virgin is being borne to heaven in terms of light and shade and moving planes.

The influence of El Greco was surprisingly limited. His son Jorge Manuel copied and imitated him; Luis Tristán probably worked in his atelier and is at any rate known to have collaborated with Jorge Manuel. But, although Tristán borrowed from El Greco types and compositions, as in the *Trinity,* he was not profoundly influenced by him, and his style was that of an eclectic in whom all the changing idioms of his time, from mannerism to naturalism, were reflected. El Greco, Spanish as he was in so many ways, did not provide a style in which Spanish artists could express themselves freely, and it was only in the new century that a completely Spanish style was evolved. The principal characteristic of this new style was naturalism, which had already expressed itself as brutal realism in earlier Spanish art and was particularly acceptable to the national temperament; it was this style which, with modifications, was to become the language used by all the greatest Spanish painters of the age.

The origins of naturalism in Spain are very obscure. Caravaggio, one of whose important gifts to baroque painting was naturalistic representation, seems almost certainly to have played a leading part with his followers in the development of Spanish painting at the beginning of the XVIIth century. Probably one of the earliest disciples of Caravaggio in Spain was Juan Bautista Maino, who, though born in Milan, must, since his only known works were executed in Spain, be considered as a Spanish artist. Although he is referred to by Palomino and Ceán Bermúdez as a pupil of El Greco (and since he was in Toledo in 1611 he must at least have known El Greco's work), his style reveals very little evidence of the latter's influence. On the other hand the Caravaggesque influence is very strong, and since he may well have been in contact with Caravaggio in Italy before he went to Spain, he may possibly be one of the vehicles through which this style was introduced there. Certainly his altar for San Pedro Mártir in Toledo, which was painted as early as 1612 and yet shows a distinct Caravaggesque style, supports this supposition.

Another artist intimately connected with the beginning of naturalism in Spain was the Valencian, Francisco Ribalta, who is usually considered to be one of the main channels for the introduction of Caravaggio's influence. Ribalta already at an earlier date than Maino was making use of chiaroscuro and realistic treatment of detail in a so called « Caravaggesque » manner (his style in his earliest work of 1582 is still in a state of formation, but in his paintings in Alegemesí of 1603 it is fully developed). But Ribalta, contrary to tradition, appears never to have been in Italy, and to have learnt his art in the Escorial. The question therefore arises, and has not yet been solved, as to whether this early phase of naturalism was not due to a general trend of artistic style developing at the beginning of the XVIIth century (the use of chiaroscuro was already developed in a similar manner by Navarrete) rather than to direct influence from Caravaggio.

The new style which marks the beginning of the XVIIth century, whether it was to a greater or lesser extent due to the influence of Caravaggio, was one of the fruits of the Counter-Reformation in its relation to art. In Italy and oher Caholic countries as a result of the Counter-Reformation the Church took up again the direction of art, which she had abandoned during the Renaissance. In Spain the influence of the Church had never slackened. After the last session of the Council of Trent, at which the Holy Council forbade the placing in churches of « any image inspired by erroneous dogma and which might lead the simple astray », and desired that « all impurity be avoided, that images should not be given provocative attractions », the Church prohibited the representation of the nude in religious art; but in Spain this again was hardly necessary, for with scarcely any exception representations of the nude were not to be found in earlier Spanish painting or sculpture. In Spain, then, the effect of the Counter-Reformation was to intensify the Church's control of art, and in particular through the Jesuit Order. The Church, which until the end of the XVth century had fought to preserve the Catholic faith against the Mohammedans, was now called upon to fight the heresies of Protestantism, and art was used as one of the chief media for propaganda. The Church prescribed the subjects to be treated by the artist and controlled the manner of representation by appointing special officers of the Inquisition to inspect works of art. The baroque, the language of the Catholic reform, by its emphasis on the visual appearance of things and on unity of effect, well fulfilled the new requirements of the Church, to convince by means of an intensely concentrated impression. Ignatius Loyola, the founder of the Jesuit Order, in his « Spiritual Exercises », instructed Christians to meditate on events in the life of Christ somewhat in the manner of an artist, to apply their senses one after the other to the subject for contemplation. Painting therefore could be one of the greatest stimuli to the exercitant of the « Spiritual Exercices »; in this capacity the greater the illusion of reality the greater the effect produced and for this end the naturalistic style was peculiarly appropriate.

Jusepe Ribera, who was certainly of Valencian origin, and possibly a pupil of Ribalta, in spite of the fact that he spent most of his life abroad, remained an essentially Spanish artist, and was the antithesis to El Greco, who, of foreign origin, was transformed into a Spanish artist through his life in Spain. Nothing at all is known of Ribera's activity in Spain. By 1616, when he was twenty-five years old, he was established in Naples and appears to have remained there until his death in 1652. His early style was strongly influenced by Caravaggio although it is not likely that he ever came into contact with him (Caravaggio died in 1610), but only with his works and with his followers.

Like Caravaggio, Ribera was reputed to have been a person of violent and revolutionary character, and something of this character does appear in his work. The scenes of martyrdom for which he is perhaps best known (the *Martyrdom of St. Bartholomew,* in the Prado, is one of the earliest examples) were well suited to be represented in the Caravaggesque style, in which the use of chiaroscuro for violent dramatic effect, the realistic treatment of detail and the selection of popular types to accentuate the actuality of the scene, gave full emphasis to the purpose for which these scenes were painted : to encourage, by glorifying the martyrs and by making familiar scenes of torture and of death, those missionaries sent by the Church to combat heresy and who were required to look for no greater glory for themselves than death by martyrdom.

Ribera was one of the few Spanish artists to represent mythological subjects, and the fact that he did so was undoubtedly due to the influence of the country in which he lived; but except for the substitution of more youthful and less coarse types, such a picture as the *Apollo and Marsyas* is not far removed in feeling from his martyrdoms of saints. Although in his early works Ribera was a « tenebrist » working in the style of Caravaggio, he gradually abandoned the artificialities of tenebrism, and developed from a painter of light and shade to a painter of light and atmosphere. In the *Communion of the Apostles,* painted in 1651, one year before his death, which sums up the whole of his achievement, the mere expression of form by contrast of light and shade has been abandoned in the pursuit of the quality of light and its relation to form.

The intensification of the religious function of art in the XVIIth century coincided with the intensification of the social aspect of court life, and caused an inevitable cleavage between religious and court art. The centre of court life from the beginning of the century was Madrid and the most important religious centre was Seville, where the precepts of the Counter-Reformation were defended with particular energy and the new saints — most of them Spanish, and many of them of Sevillian origin — were the objects of special devotion. Francisco Pacheco, though an artist of little merit, is important in so far as he represents academic authority and the influence of the Church. He began his career by painting in the current mannerist style of Seville. In 1611 he went to Madrid and Toledo where he met El Greco. On his return to Seville, Pacheco opened a school of painting where amongst others Velázquez received his early training. In 1618 he was appointed official art censor by the Holy Office. In his « Arte de la Pintura », Pacheco set the standard for æsthetic appreciation, and laid down rules of decorum. Although he extolled Michelangelo and Raphael as the greatest of all painters he also recognized the merits of Caravaggio. « I keep to nature in everything and if only it were possible to keep it always before one's eyes at every moment, not only for heads, nudes, hands and feet, but also for draperies, silks and everything else, it would be best. In this way Michelangelo Caravaggio worked... and with what success ! »

As an artist, however, Pacheco was more conservative than as a theorist, although he made some attempt to paint directly from nature, as in the *Portrait of a Donor,* it remained for his pupil Velázquez to develop to perfection this new manner. His *Immaculate Conception,* painted according to the formula Pacheco himself laid down in his « Arte de la Pintura », that the Virgin should be represented « in the flower of her age, from twelve to thirteen years old, with sweet grave eyes, a nose and mouth of the most perfect hue... in a word, with all the beauty that a pencil can portray » provided the model for the innumerable *Purísimas* that abound in Seville, where more than anywhere else in Spain the dogma of the Immaculate Conception was upheld. Pacheco represented the Virgin surrounded by the symbols of the litany, and adored by the poet Miguel Cid, author of verses in honour of the Immaculate Conception.

The artists who represented in Seville the transition from mannerism to naturalism announced by Pacheco, were Juan de las Roelas and Francisco Herrera the Elder. In both artists can be traced the development from the type of mannerist composition to the baroque and to a broader technique. Roelas' insistence on naturalistic details in the accessory figures of his religious compositions heralded the genre compositions which were so popular in Seville in the XVIIth century and in which such figures alone provided the subject matter of a picture. Herrera was conservative in his use of mannerist types and compositions, but in his naturalistic style and coarse, painterly technique he was a product of the new century; his realistic treatment of detail is exaggerated to the point of distortion. Both Roelas, who was a prebendary of the Church, and Herrera, worked almost exclusively for the Church.

The artist who expressed the precepts of the Church — the Church of the Counter-Reformation — more powerfully and sensitively than any other artist in Andalusia or indeed in any other part of Spain was Francisco Zurbarán, who was active most of his life in Seville. He was also primarily a religious painter and in sincere devoutness and religious fervour he was a direct successor to Morales and El Greco. Zurbarán was one of the Spanish artists in whom the Caravaggesque influence was most clearly manifested, and his style, though partly derived from Ribera, whose works began to appear in Spain from about 1616 onward, looked back in its purity and intensity to the capo-scuola himself rather than to his followers. Like Caravaggio he used chiaroscuro for the definition of form and for dramatic effect and his simplicity of composition and clarity of design seem the expression of a personal simplicity. His emphasis on the naturalistic aspects of his subject and his simplifications of form show his work to be in particularly close sympathy with the teachings of Loyola's « Spiritual Exercices », where the exercitant is instructed to intensify contemplation by application of the senses. Zurbarán represents saints and religious scenes in a direct manner which leaves little to the imagination, and his textures have always a peculiarly tactile quality. A further connection with the « Exercices » can be traced in the subject matter of Zurbarán's paintings, as for instance in his conception of *St. Francis in meditation*, of which an example is in the National Gallery. Meditation on death, according to St. Ignatius, should be made in a darkened room, for obscurity aids the impression of horror, and further, the meditator must have within view a skull or some other image of death. Zurbarán represented St. Francis with such naturalism that this picture and other versions have been thought to be portraits of Franciscan monks; and, indeed, it was no doubt the aim of the artist, in the spirit of the « Exercises », to encourage the worshipper to identify himself with the saint and to recapture his emotions.

The altar-piece of St. Peter in Seville cathedral, in which Ribera's influence is proved by the connection of the scene of the *Tears of St. Peter* with a Ribera etching, was Zurbarán's first important commission. The cult of St. Peter as the first Pope and as patron of confession was particularly favoured by the Catholic Church and his representation frequent in the XVIIth century as a counterblast against its condemnation by the Protestants. In the important series of paintings executed in 1638-39 for the sacristy of the Jeronymite monastery of Guadalupe, Zurbarán represents members of the Order in moments of vision or ecstacy, and St. Jerome, the founder, is shown in the scenes of his Temptation and Flagellation (the second representing a dream in which the Saint was ordered to be whipped by angels for reading Cicero instead of the Prophets). In 1658 Zurbarán went to Madrid, probably for the first time. From this date, apparently as a result of his contact with the court, he abandoned his earlier simplicity and clarity, and late works, such as the *Immaculate Conception* of 1661 lack the vigour and sincerity of those executed when he was confined to more provincial surroundings.

Born a year after Zurbarán and educated in the same artistic milieu, Diego

Velázquez also began his career as a provincial artist, but unlike Zurbarán he went to Madrid at an early age and developed through contact with the court. The two principal patrons of art in the Spain of this time were still the church and the court; Zurbarán had found his métier in the employ of the former, Velázquez found his in that of the latter. He probably studied for a short period under Herrera, whom he was forced to quit, according to tradition, on account of his master's violent temper. He then entered the studio of Pacheco for five years and his studies there set him in the direction which he was to follow throughout his career. Pacheco emphasized the need for an artist always to have a model before him and praised Velázquez because he « worked from life, making numerous studies of his model in various poses, and thereby he gained certainty in his portraits ». From this interest in the study from nature, as advocated by Pacheco and practized in his school, was derived a genre of painting particularly popular in Spain, and more especially in Seville, during the first half of the XVIIth century, namely the « bodegón » (1), and Velázquez was, it seems, one of the first artists to develop it. His *Christ in the house of Martha* (National Gallery), one of his earliest works, is to all intents and purposes a « bodegón », since most attention is given to the painting of the humble figures and the still-life in the foreground although as in analogous compositions in Dutch prototypes the religious scene is enacted in the background and provides the « raison d'être » of the painting. In other « bodegones » of his Sevillian period Velázquez dispensed with this religious motive altogether. The *Portrait of Dona Gerónima de la Fuente,* in which every plane is carefully modelled in light and shade, illustrates what Pacheco meant when he said that by his study of the model Velázquez « gained certainty in his portraiture ». Pacheco's own attempts in this direction, his *Portrait of a donor,* for example, reveals only a literal annotation of facts.

Velázquez's object from the beginning of his career was to represent his model as he saw it and his artistic development was engendered by the development of his vision. His first step was to represent his model piece by piece as he saw it; his final achievement was the representation of the visual appearance of a figure or scene as a whole. In his early works he modelled in light and shade in the manner of Caravaggio and like Caravaggio gave equal importance to still-life and to figures, but the result was essentially different, less dramatic and less emotional. In Velázquez there are no violent contrasts of light and shade, nothing is lost in dark shadow, but every passage is equally worked out. For whereas Caravaggio did not actually develop chiaroscuro beyond « theatrical verisimilitude », Velázquez used it only as a first step in his statement of objective vision.

In 1622 Velázquez paid his first visit to Madrid, desirous, according to Pacheco, of seeing the Escorial, but in all probability with the hope of attaching himself to the court. He returned there in 1623, met with complete recognition and was established at the court for the rest of his life, working in the service of Philip IV who had come to the throne at the age of fourteen

(1). « Bodegón » is the Spanish word for a tavern or drinking-booth, and is applied to pictures of them, and, by extension, to still-life subjects in which comestibles are represented.

only two years previously. Philip IV, like his grandfather Philip II, was always in close personal contact with his artists, and did not fail to influence their production. « His epoch, so saddened by political failures and financial maladministration, has otherwise a far more *Spanish complexion* than earlier times, and the art of Velázquez had a more truly Spanish character than that of any artist of this or any previous epoch.

In his first years at Madrid he devoted himself almost entirely to portraiture, adapting the naturalistic style that he had learned in Seville to the conventions of court portraiture, conventions which had been to a considerable extent modified by the sumptuary laws of 1623. The new fashions in dress, at least for men, were subdued and simple, and simplicity was the keynote of Velázquez's early court portraits — simplicity in the representation of plastic effect and of light; with colour he was so far comparatively little concerned.

In 1628 Rubens visited Madrid; his visit marked the beginning of a new stage in Velázquez's development, due, however, less to any direct pictorial influence of Rubens — although his influence on the rest of the Madrid school was immense — than to the stimulus provided by Rubens' art. The really important factor in his development at this time was his journey to Italy in the following year, and the most important event in that journey was his contact with the work of the great Venetian painters of the preceding century. Whilst in Italy he painted the *Forge of Vulcan* (Prado) and *Jacob receiving Joseph's coat* (Escorial), which, in contrast with the *Borrachos* (Prado) painted just before his departure, mark his emancipation from the limitations of Caravaggesque naturalism and an advance in understanding of space and atmosphere and colour. On his return to Madrid after a two years' absence, Velázquez still gave himself almost entirely to portraiture, and his portraits of this period show an increased freedom of technique and richer tonality; his interest in light was no longer confined to its relation to form alone, but also to its spatial and colouristic implications. In these years he also painted a series of court portraits for the decoration of the Buen Retiro Palace, and for the Salón de Reinos he executed one of his most superb compositions, the *Surrender of Breda,* which sums up the whole of his artistic achievement at this date. The motive of the two generals — the victorious and the conquered — besides formally uniting the composition has an emotional content which is rare in Velázquez.

In 1649 Velázquez returned to Italy, this time to buy works of art for Philip, and his *Portrait of Pope Innocent X,* painted in Rome in 1650, shows him to be already embarked on the last phase of his achievement of visual truth. Back in Madrid he continued to paint the King and his court. The comparison of a portrait of Philip of this last phase with an early portrait of the King reveals the distance the artist had travelled from « terre-à-terre » realism to spiritual vision — from composition with nearly equal stress on every feature, to the representation of visual appearance where all detail is subordinated to the general effect. In his late portraits of the Queen and the Infantas all detailed description is abandoned even in the richly decorated dresses, but the impression of their elaborate details is truthfully rendered with rich and subtle harmony of colour.

Velázquez's production was by no means confined to portraiture — it included religious and mythological compositions and landscape in which his stylistic development was not less evident nor of less significance than in his portraits — but he was first and foremost a court painter; almost his sole patron was the King, and his art reflected the apogee of royal despotism in Spain.

Velázquez had many imitators and followers but few pupils, and there was no artist in Spain until Goya, a century and a half later, capable of carrying on from where he left off. Of the crowd of mediocre painters working in Madrid who imitated his style the two most important were his son-in-law, Juan Bautista del Mazo, and Juan Carreño de Miranda; the former worked in his studio, often in collaboration with him, and succeeded him as first court painter on his death; the latter was also court painter to Philip IV and later to Charles II. Both artists carried on the tradition of court portraiture and to a certain extent imitated Velázquez's technical achievements. Carreño, however, in his later work tended towards the exaggerated elegance of posture and fluency of technique which marked the transition from Philip's reign to that of his successor.

Although Philip IV was by no means less fervent a Catholic than his predecessors, his reign marked the separation of court art from religious art. The King no longer identified himself with the Church, but whilst the production of court artists became more and more confined to portraiture and the decoration of royal dwellings, the activity of the Church as patron of art in no way diminished. Fray Juan Rizi, a pupil of Maino and contemporary of Velázquez, worked principally for the Benedictine Order, of which he himself was a member. In Valencia Jerónimo Jacinto Espinosa, a follower of Ribalta, filled churches and monasteries with large altar-pieces devoted especially to the propaganda of Counter-Reformation. Alonso Cano, born in Granada, and later prebendary of the cathedral there, was like Velázquez a pupil of Pacheco in Seville and was educated in the naturalistic style. In 1628 he went to Madrid, and, as a result of the influence of the works of earlier and contemporary masters he saw at the court, developed an eclectic style, but his paintings always possess a strong plastic quality, due no doubt to the fact that he was also, and primarily, a sculptor.

In Seville increasing commercial prosperity went with increasing religious devotion, and the most popular interpretation of this religious devotion was Francisco Murillo In contrast to Zurbarán, whose paintings were for the most part intended to appeal to the clergy and the majority of whose works were in monastic establishments, Murillo painted mostly for the layman; his paintings were intended to be hung in places of public worship, and this accounts to a great extent for their essentially popular character. Whereas Zurbarán emphasized the ascetic and monastic character of religious scenes, Murillo accentuated their human and popular side. He rarely depicted scenes of martyrdom or saints in ecstasy, subjects intended to inspire the clergy, but concentrated on the representation of the more popular religious subjects in terms of everyday life, and in particular of everyday life in Seville, taking for his models characteristic local types. Amongst his chief patrons, moreover, were the Franciscans whose principle of faith was humility and whose saints had attained glory through simple acts of faith and charity. The *Charity of St. Diego,* one of Murillo's earliest known works, represents the Franciscan saint in monk's garb in the act of distributing food to a group of poor people, and is executed in the naturalistic tradition of Pacheco and the young Velázquez.

In the *St. Francis embracing Christ on the Cross,* a late work painted for the Capucines at Seville, and obviously inspired by Ribalta's painting in Valencia, the founder of the order is represented in mystic conversation with Christ, symbolizing the union of man with God. Here in his fully developed style Murillo continued to translate a superhuman element into human terms, but no longer according to his early method of literal realism. For the expression of his popular sentimentality he developed a more fluid technique and an artificial system of lighting which gave to his religious scenes an unearthly character by means of vaporous clouds and the radiation of a luminous aura around his figures.

Most numerous of all the subjects depicted by Murillo were his representations of the Immaculate Conception, a dogma which still enjoyed special devotion in Seville, and of which Murillo provided the most popular interpretation. The creation of popular types of religious figures, and the interest in genre manifested in his religious compositions, as for instance in the *Miracle of Moses,* led Murillo to create a new type of genre composition, the scene with beggar children, in which he transformed the realistic children and beggars of the early Sevillan « bodegón » into an idealized and « picturesque » popular type not far removed from his angels and cherubs — different indeed in conception from Ribera's *Clubfoot,* and farther still from Velázquez's purely objective studies of dwarfs.

Valdés Leal, who in 1660 assisted Murillo in founding an academy of painting in Seville, was the embodiment of the late and decadent stage of the baroque in religious art. In the place of the clarity and severe dignity of Zurbarán and the sentimental serenity of Murillo he produced by means of violence of movement and wildness of gesture, aided by harsh discordant colour, exaggerated dramatic effects, which reflected yet another aspect of XVIIth century Roman Catholicism — its tendency to evoke violent emotion as an instrument of policy. In the *Flagellation of St. Jerome,* in contrast to the version of this subject by Zurbarán in which the Saint is represented looking up with an expression of rapt devotion to the figure of Christ, St. Jerome is bowed down in passionate despair whilst an angel is in the act of flogging him.

In the two *Allegories of Death,* painted for the Hospital de la Caridad in Seville, Valdés Leal was called upon to interpret the contemplations on death of the founder of the Hospital, Miguel de Mañara, a Sevillian nobleman who has been identified with the legendary figure of Don Juan, and who after leading a life of debauchery was converted to Catholicism and devoted the rest of his life to religious meditation. The allegories were intended as a warning to those who die without grace or hope of salvation, for whom death must mean « dust and ashes, corruption and worms, the tomb and oblivion ».

Murillo died in 1682 and Valdés Leal in 1690; the former had numerous imitators and followers though none of note; the style of the latter reached its last stage of decadence in the work of his son Lucas Valdés. In

Madrid the last years of the Habsburg dynasty, which ended with the reign of Charles II at the end of the century, saw an exaggerated development of the baroque, parallel to that of Valdés Leal, in the production of Cerezo and Cabezalero, pupils of Carreño, and of Juan Rizi and Herrera the Younger. The last master of the school of Madrid was Claudio Coello, who alone succeeded in giving to this style some expression of dignity. His *Charles II adoring the Host*, in the Escorial, is as complete an expression of the baroque — the picture being conceived as a continuation of the room in which it hangs — as Velázquez's *Maids of Honour*.

Already in Claudio Coello's life-time Charles II had summoned to his court the Neapolitan Luca Giordano, the first of a series of foreign artists who were to monopolize the production of painting at the Spanish court during the XVIIIth century, and Spanish painting began to resolve itself into a mediocre echo of the production of the late XVIIth century. In 1713, as a result of the War of the Spanish Succession, the Bourbon Philip V came to the throne and with him began the introduction of French influence in every aspect of court life. The baroque gave place to French rococo. The French artists Michel-Ange Houasse, Jean Ranc and Louis-Michel Vanloo were invited to Madrid to be court painters to Philip V; they were followed by the Italians Jacopo Amigoni and Corrado Giaquinto. In 1751 an Academy of Art was founded in Madrid (Corrado Giaquinto was appointed director of painting), which standardized the production of the next years. A few years later the Academy instituted pensions to Rome where the most promising Spanish artists were sent to be trained. In 1761 the German artist Anton Raphael Mengs, a close friend of Winkelmann whose writings did much to further the neo-classical style, went to Madrid where he was made director of the Academy and court painter to Charles III. Two years later Giambattista Tiepolo arrived in Madrid with his two sons, and worked there until his death in 1770, the year before Mengs left Madrid. Both artists were employed by the King on the decoration of the Royal Palace, but Tiepolo was overshadowed by Mengs, and it was Mengs, the highest exponent of academic classicism, who as director of all the artistic activity at the court, was responsible for the training of the new generation of Spanish artists from which came Francisco Goya.

Goya was born in 1746 near Saragossa and died in 1828 in Bordeaux. His life covered a period of political and social change which was reflected in his art. He was at the beginning of his career a product of his age — an eclectic product of the combined influences of Giaquinto, Mengs, Tiepolo and Francisco Bayeu, which resulted in a mixture of rococo and neo-classicism. Like Velázquez, Goya was court painter during most of his life-time, but unlike Velázquez, he was by no means dependent on the King alone as patron. He worked for members of the court and the wealthier middle classes, and he also produced a large number of works independent of any patron in which, to quote Goya himself, he was able « to make observations for which commissioned works generally give no room, and in which fantasy and invention have no limit ». Thus in Goya can be traced a dual development, that of the official painter and that of the free artist, and it is as the latter that his personality found fullest expression. His first official commission for the court was a series of cartoons for tapestries intended for the decoration of the royal palaces, begun in 1776 and executed in collaboration with Francisco and Ramón Bayeu, José Castillo and other Spanish artists, at first under the direction of Mengs, later under that of his brother-in-law, the elder Bayeu. The subjects vary from scenes reflecting the most exaggerated aspects of aristocratic court life to genre scenes of a popular character.

In 1785 Goya was appointed sub-director of the Academy of San Fernando; he had already embarked on his career as a portraitist and was painting portraits in an official academic style. In 1789 he attained the long-desired position of court painter to Charles IV, who had come to the throne in the previous year and whose reign marked a period of reaction against the comparatively enlightened rule of Charles III. Charles IV, on the eve of the French Revolution, introduced a new era of extravagant court life, and of political intrigue. In 1793 he declared war on the new French Republic, but in Spain the growing need for social reform saw a number of sympathizers with the revolution. Goya despite his increasingly close connection with court circles — in 1795 he became director of the Academy and in 1799 first painter to the King — reflected the abuses of the society in which he lived with such truth and powerful sincerity that even his official portraits of the King and Queen by their satirical realism do not fail to record his censure. His most outspoken criticism was embodied in the *Caprichos,* a series of etchings in which he condemned by satire all the political, social and religious corruption of his day. In every field of his art Goya applied his increasingly subjective vision, in religious, decorative and genre compositions, in official portraits and portraits of his friends, and as in the case of Velázquez, with the development of his vision, his style developed increasingly towards a sublimated rendering of the visual appearance of things.

In 1808, as a result of a series of political intrigues, the King abdicated in favour of his son Ferdinand VII, who, however, in the same year was forced to flee on the entry of the Napoleonic army into Spain. Joseph Bonaparte was crowned king, but although he reigned at the court and was even welcomed by many as representing liberalism in opposition to the despotism of Charles, the Spanish people rose against the foreign invader, and after a war which lasted six years the French were forced to leave. Goya officially accepted the new régime and received the Royal Order of Spain from the French king, but his personal attitude towards the invasion is seen clearly in the *3rd of May* 1808, a scene representing the execution by French soldiers of the defenders of Madrid. This is no glorification of the war theme, but an impersonal, non-heroic account of an event seen, depicted in a powerful narrative style. His power of direct reporting was more definitely revealed in the *Disasters of War,* a series of etchings recording common occurences during the War of Independence, which by reason of their brutal objectivity constitute the most moving invective against war.

In 1814 the French finally retired and Ferdinand VII returned to the throne, inaugurating a period of intense reaction. Goya, in spite of having served the French king, received Ferdinand's pardon and was even appointed court painter. Yet his portraits of Ferdinand so truly and so forcefully reflect the personality of this King, an arrogant though weak and insignificant-looking man, that as in the case of his portraits of Charles IV and his Queen it seems incredible that the artist was not condemned for his outspokenness in representing him as he really appeared. Besides official portraits Goya continued to paint more intimate portraits of friends as well as scenes or people that interested him, of which the *Head of a Monk* is a typical example, and in which he tended towards ever greater breadth of vision and a consequently increasingly impressionistic style.

As a religious painter Goya had in his early frescoes in Saragossa followed the recipes of rococo decoration; in the *Capture of Christ* he developed all the dramatic possibilities of the scene in a Rembrandtesque manner; in his etchings he criticized with overwhelming force the abuses of the Church; in the *Communion of St. José of Calasanz,* which was commissioned in 1819 for the church of the Escuelas Pías, he reveals an attitude of sincere religious devotion comparable only to that of the religious painters of Spain of the XVIIth century. For Goya, though he condemned the abuses of the Church as he condemned all social and political abuses, never showed disrespect towards religion and was throughout his life a sincerely religious man.

In 1824, when the collapse of an attempt to establish a liberal government produced an even more violent reaction than that of 1814, Goya abandoned the court and Spain and went into voluntary exile in France, where a number of his friends had already preceded him. Though by this time old, ill and stone deaf, he continued to paint and to etch with increasing enthusiasm until his death in 1828. « Everything fails me, only my will survives », he wrote to a friend towards the end of his life. He was the greatest artistic personality of his age, in whose single personality were foreshadowed the artistic developments of the new century, and his evolution was unique : his masters were the late XVIIIth century academicians, his heirs the French masters of the XIXth century. He was, too, the last great Spanish artist; after him painting in Spain sank into complete insignificance.

THE ARTISTS

Alfonso, *Master* (op. 1473).

In 1473 a Master Alfonso painted a series of panels from the life of St. Cucufas for the church of San Cugat del Vallés, near Barcelona. The « Martyrdom of Cucufas (?) » in the Barcelona Museum is identified as one of this series because of its subject, provenance and approximate date. The artist is probably to be identified with Alfonso de Córdoba who in 1465 received payment for work in the Royal Chapel of the Constable, Barcelona.

Bassa, Ferrer (op. 1325-m. 1348).

Catalan painter and miniaturist; active in the kingdom of Aragon. First documented in 1324 when he was paid for the decoration of two chapels at Sitges (no longer extant). 1333-34 engaged on the illumination of a manuscript entitled « Usatges de Barcelona y Costums de Catalunya » for King Alfonso IV of Aragon. Commissions for various works for Peter IV who came to the throne in 1336 are also recorded. His only certain extant works are the fresco decorations of the Chapel of San Miguel in the Franciscan Convent of Pedralbes, near Barcelona, executed 1345-1346, representing scenes from the Passion and from the life of the Virgin and twelve figures of Saints. The strong Florentine and Sienese influences suggest that he must very probably have studied in Italy. Died in 1348 while executing an altar for the Franciscan Monastery in Valencia.

Bayeu y Subías, Francisco (1734-1795).

Born in Saragossa in 1734. Studied under José Luzán who was later Goya's first teacher. In Madrid he studied under Antonio González Velázquez; he worked for Charles III in the decoration of the royal palace, under the direction of Mengs. Some time before 1771 Goya was his pupil, and he supervised Goya's early decorations in Saragossa. 1777 he succeeded Mengs as art director of the tapestry factory of Santa Bárbara. 1788 he was appointed director of the Academy of San Fernando and court painter to Charles IV. Died in Madrid in 1795.

Bayeu y Subías, Ramón (1746-1793).

Brother of Francisco Bayeu. Born in Saragossa in 1746. Studied in the Academy of San Fernando, Madrid. 1766 he won a first prize in a competition for which Goya also entered, but without success. 1776 engaged by Mengs to paint tapestry cartoons; 1780 he worked with Goya on the decorations for Saragossa Cathedral. Died in 1793.

Bermejo, Bartolomé (op. 1474-1495).

His real name was Bartolomé de Cárdenas but he is usually referred to, and signed himself, as Bartolomé Bermejo or Rubeus. From the adjective « cordubensis » in the signature of his « Pietà », it may be assumed that he was of Cordobese origin. First documented in 1474 in Daroca. By 1486 established in Barcelona. 1490 finished the « Pietà », painted for Luis Desplá, Canon of the Cathedral. One of the first artists to introduce oil painting into Spain; his contracts from 1475 stipulate this medium. Last recorded in Barcelona in 1495.

Berruguete, Pedro (op. 1483 - m. 1503 /4).

Born in Castile. Court painter to Ferdinand and Isabella. Probably worked in Avila. 1483 active in Toledo, where he executed the wall-paintings in the sacristy of the Cathedral in collaboration with Master Antonio (Antonio del Rincón ?). There is little doubt that he is to be identified with the « Pietro Spagnuolo », who in 1477 was working in Urbino on the decoration of the library of the Duke Frederico, together with Melozza da Forli and Justus of Ghent. Died before January 6th 1504.

Borrassá, Luis (op. 1388-1424).

He can perhaps be identified with a painter of the same name referred to in a document of 1380 as being employed to repair glass windows in Gerona Cathedral. Probably a pupil of Pedro Serra. 1388 established in Barcelona. From this date contracts for altars for churches in Barcelona and neighbouring towns exist until 1424, the last date in which he is recorded.

CANO, Alonso (1601-1667).

Architect, sculptor and painter; born in Granada in 1601. Went to Seville about 1616 where he studied painting under Juan del Castillo, Pacheco and Herrera, and sculpture under Montañés. From 1634-1644 active in Madrid. Then, accused of the murder of his wife, he fled to Valencia, returning later to Madrid. 1651 he was made prebendary of Granada Cathedral. From 1658 to 1660 he was again in Madrid, then returned to Granada where he died in 1667.

CARDUCHO, Vicente (1576-1638).

Born in 1576 in Florence. He went to Spain at an early age with his brother Bartolomé, whom he succeeded as court painter to Philip III in 1609. 1633 he published the « Dialogos de la Pintura », a treatise of painting. Assisted in the decoration of the Salon de Reinos in the Buen Retiro. He defended the plea for exemption from taxation of painters, which was finally successful in 1637. Died in Madrid in 1638.

CARREÑO DE MIRANDA, Juan (1614-1685).

Born in Avilés in 1614. 1623 he went to Madrid, where he studied under Pedro de las Cuevas and Bartolomé Román. He was introduced to the Court by Velázquez and in 1669 was made painter to the king and in 1671 court painter to Charles II. He executed a large number of court portraits, religious compositions and fresco decorations. Died in Madrid in 1685.

CASTILLO, José del (1737-1793).

Born in Madrid in 1737; studied in Rome under Giaquinto and returned with him to Madrid in 1753. 1764 on his return to Madrid after a second visit to Rome he was employed to paint cartoons for the tapestry factory of Santa Bárbara, under the direction of Mengs, later of Francisco Bayeu, and worked on the same series of cartoons as Goya, etc. 1785 honorary member of the Academy, then sub-director. Died in Madrid in 1793.

COELLO, Claudio (1642-1693).

Born in Madrid in 1642; he studied under Francisco Rizi. 1671 in collaboration with José Donoso executed the fresco decorations in the vestry of Toledo Cathedral. 1683 active in Saragossa. 1685 court painter to Charles II. Executed decorations for churches and public buildings in Madrid. 1691 painter to the Cathedral of Toledo. Died in Madrid in 1693.

DALMAU, Luis (op. 1428-1460).

1428 recorded as a painter of Valencia; received payment for expenses for a journey to Castile on behalf of Alfonso V of Aragon to whom he was court painter. 1431 sent by the king to Flanders. 1437 back in Valencia. His only certain extant work is the « Virgin with the Councillors », an altarpiece executed in 1443-45 for the chapel of the Municipal Council in Barcelona; largely adapted from compositions by Van Eyck. 1453 recorded as a painter and citizen of Barcelona.1460 last documented as working for the new king Juan II.

ESPINOSA, Jerónimo Jacinto (1600-1667).

Born in Concentaina in 1600. Probably studied in Valencia under Francisco Ribalta; at any rate he was strongly influenced by him. He executed a large number of religious compositions for churches and monasteries in the province of Valencia. Died in Valencia in 1667.

FERNÁNDEZ, Alejo (op. 1498-m. 1543).

First documented in Cordova in 1498. He is the most important artist working in Andalusia during the first part of the XVth century; worked principally in Cordova and Seville, although commissioned for works for other parts of Spain. 1508 in Seville. His « Vírgen del Buen Aire » (c. 1520), representing the Virgin as protector of merchants, was painted for the Chapel of the Spanish Colonial Ministry, the centre of commerce with America. Also worked as miniaturist. 1526 superintended the decorations in Seville for the entry of Charles V. Died in Seville in 1543.

GALLEGO, Fernando (op. 1468-1507).

First documented as working in the Cathedral of Plasencia in 1468. From this date he was active in Castile, particularly in Salamanca and Zamora, and proved a very prolific artist with considerable influence on his contemporaries in this part of Spain. Gallego worked in oils and was strongly influenced by Flemish painting particularly by Dierick Bouts; he also derived several of his compositions from Schongauer engravings. Died after 1507, the last date in which he is documented.

Goya y Lucientes, Francisco (1746-1828).

1746 born in Fuendetodos, near Saragossa. 1760 in Saragossa; studied painting for six years with José Luzán. 1771 in Rome; won the second prize for a competition held by the Academy of Parma, mentioned as pupil of Francisco Bayeu. In the same year began decorations of Saragossa Cathedral. 1775-1776 in Madrid. 1776 began work on tapestry cartoons. 1780 failed to gain position as court painter, but elected member of the Academy of San Fernando. Continued work on decorations in Saragossa. 1781 returned to Madrid. 1785 appointed sub-director of the Academy; series of official portraits. 1789 court painter to Charles IV. 1792 long illness which left him deaf. 1795 replaced Bayeu as director of the Academy; 1797 after an absence from Madrid resigned directorship. 1798 decorations for the church of S. Antonio de la Florida, in Madrid. 1799 Announcement of sale of the « Caprichos » (etchings). Made first court painter. 1808 Charles abdicated; portrait of the new king Ferdinand VII. 1808-1814 French invasion and War of Independence. Began series of etchings entitled « Disasters of War ». 1811 received Royal Order of Spain from the king, Joseph Bonaparte. 1814 Ferdinand returned; Goya accepted by him, and continued to paint official portraits. 1819 first lithographs; illness and production of « Disparates » (etchings). 1823 White Terror in Madrid. 1824 Goya went to France. Visited Paris and settled in Bordeaux. 1826 returned to Madrid for a few months. 1828 died in Bordeaux.

Herrera, Francisco, the Elder (1576-c. 1656).

Born in Seville in 1576. According to Ceán Bermúdez he studied, with Pacheco, under Luis Fernández. Worked in Seville most of his life, and was for a short period the master of Velázquez (c. 1611-1612). 1627 he collaborated with Zurbarán on a series of Pictures for the Colegio de San Buenaventura. Went to Madrid towards the end of his life, where he probably died in 1656.

Jacomart (Jaime Baço), 1409 / 17-1461.

Born in 1409/17 in Valencia. 1442 court painter to Alfonso V of Aragon who summoned him to Naples. 1447 with Alfonso at Tivoli. By 1451 he was back in Valencia. 1460 court painter to John II who succeeded Alfonso. To this year belongs the document for the retable of Catí, but the work has now, for stylistic reasons, been ascribed to Juan Rexach and the problem of the identification of the work of Jacomart and Rexach remains to be solved. There are in fact no definitely authenticated works by Jacomart; yet there is evidence to show that he was the principle figure in the production of painting in Valencia during the third quarter of the XVth century. Died in 1561 in Valencia.

Juanes, Juan de (Vicente Juan Masip), (c. 1505/23-1579).

Born near Valencia possibly c. 1505 or according to early biographers in 1523. Son and pupil of Vicente Masip, whose later work is easily confused with the son's. Worked in Valencia, where he had a number of followers; strongly influenced by Italian painting. Died in 1579 in Bocariente.

Maella, Mariano (1739-1819).

Born in Valencia in 1739. Studied in the Academy of San Fernando, which was under the directorship of Corrado Giaquinto. Worked for several years in Rome; on his return to Spain he worked under the direction of Mengs; 1774 he was made court painter, in 1782 sub-director of the Academy, in 1794 director (the next year Goya was appointed sub-director under him). 1799 he became first court painter to Charles IV; like Goya he maintained his position during the reign of Joseph Bonaparte, and was presented with the Royal Order of Spain and was also accepted by Ferdinand VII on his restoration. Died in Madrid in 1819, considered the most distinguished academic painter of his time.

Maino, Juan Bautista (c. 1586-1649).

Born near Milan before 1586. 1611 first mentioned in a document as being active in Toledo. 1612 contract for the high altar of the church of the Dominican monastery San Pedro Mártir, Toledo, and became a member of the monastery before completing it. Before 1621 he was established in Madrid as drawing master to the Infante Philip (later Philip IV). 1627 with Crescenzio he awarded a prize to Velázquez for his « Expulsion of the Moors ». By 1634 he had completed the « Recovery of the Bay of San Salvador » for the Salón de Reinos of the Buen Retiro. Died in 1649 in Madrid, in the College of Santo Tomás.

MARZAL DE SAX, Andrés (op. 1394-1410).

Active in Valencia; probably of German origin (from Saxony?). Possibly collaborated with Pedro Nicolau. The « Incredulity of St. Thomas » (Valencia Cathedral) is in all probability part of the altarpiece of St. Thomas for which the artist received payment in 1400.

MAZO, Juan Bautista Martínez del (c. 1612-1667).

Born near Cuenca; the date of his birth is not known. He studied in Madrid under Velázquez, whose daughter he married in 1634. Court painter to Philip IV. 1643-46 drawing master to the Infante Baltasar Carlos. He collaborated with Velázquez and after the latter's death succeeded him as first court painter in 1661. Died in Madrid in 1667.

MELÉNDEZ, Luis Eugenio (1716-1780).

Born in Naples, in 1716, of Spanish parents. 1717 taken to Madrid. Pupil of his father Francisco Antonio and of L.-M. van Loo. 1760 and 1772 applied unsuccessfully for position as court painter. Went to Rome and Naples; on his return to Madrid court painter to Charles III. Principally a still-life painter. Died in Madrid in 1780.

MORALES, Luis de (op. 1546-m. 1586).

Born probably in Badajoz; the date of his birth is not known. Active in Estremadura. His relations with Philip II are not documented and there is no evidence that he was employed by the king to work in the Escorial. Called by the early biographers the « divine Morales » because of the character of his religious pictures. There exist several versions of his « Christ carrying the Cross », « Pietà », « Virgin and Child », etc. Died in Badajoz in 1586.

MURILLO, Bartolomé Estéban (1617-1682).

Baptized in Seville on January 1st, 1617. Studied painting under Juan del Castillo. There is no documentary evidence for his ever having visited the Court, and he appears to have worked all his life in Seville and neighbouring towns painting chiefly for convents and churches. He was a member of the « Hermandad de la Caridad ». 1660 he founded the Academy of Painting in Seville and was its first president. Died in Seville in 1682.

NAVARRETE, Juan Fernández, *el Mudo* (c. 1526-1579).

Born in Logroño about 1526. At the age of three he became deaf and could not learn to speak. Sent to Jeronymite monastery of La Estrella where he learnt to paint. Went to Italy where he studied for several years. When over forty, back in Spain, he applied to enter the service of Philip II. 1568 appointed court painter to Philip. He painted eight altar-pieces in the Escorial, leaving the rest of the series of thirty-two unfinished at his death in 1579.

ORRENTE, Pedro (c. 1570-1645).

Born in Montealegre about 1570. He worked chiefly in Toledo, where he was in close contact with El Greco's son. 1616 active in Valencia. 1617 he received payment for the « St. Leocadia » in Toledo Cathedral. In 1641 he was in Murcia. Palomino asserts that he was an officer of the Inquisition. Died in Valencia in 1645.

PACHECO, Francisco (1564-1654).

Born in 1564 in Sanlúcar de Barrameda in Andalusia. Studied in Seville under Luis Fernández. 1611 visited Madrid and Toledo, where he met El Greco. Returned to Seville where he formed a school. 1612-1617 master of Velázquez. 1618 appointed official art censor for the Inquisition. 1623 accompanied Velázquez to Madrid, remaining there two years. 1649 he published the « Arte de la Pintura », a treatise on painting, particularly valuable for its information concerning contemporary artists. Died in Seville in 1654.

PANTOJA DE LA CRUZ, Juan (1551-1608).

Born in Madrid in 1551. Pupil and follower of Sánchez Coello. Court painter to Philip II and Philip III. Besides a large number of portraits of the royal family and court circles he also executed several religious works. Died in Madrid in 1608.

PEDRO DE CÓRDOBA (op. 1475).

Known only from the signature on the « Annunciation » in the Cathedral of Cordova, painted in 1475 for the canon Diego Sánchez de Castro. This is the only work that can with certainty be ascribed to him. The School of Cordova in the second half of the XVth century was nearly as productive as that of Seville, and is characterized by a stronger Flemish influence.

Ribalta, Francisco (1551/55-1628).

Born in Castellón de la Plana in 1551 or 1555. His « Christ nailed to the Cross » in the Hermitage is signed and dated in Madrid in 1582. Probably studied in the Escorial; his « Santiago » in Algemesí (1603) is a close adaptation of the same subject by Navarrete in the Escorial. He worked chiefly in the province of Valencia and is one of the first artists in Spain to use chiaroscuro in the manner of Caravaggio and his followers. Died in Valencia in 1628.

Ribalta, Juan (1597-1628).

Son and pupil of Francisco. Born in 1597, probably in Madrid. The date of his birth is deduced from the inscription on the « Christ nailed to the Cross» (Valencia Museum) which has been read « Joannes Ribalta pingebat et invenit 18 ætatis suæ anno 1615 ». (The inscription is no longer legible). Painted a series of portraits. Frequently collaborated with his father. Died in Valencia in 1628.

Ribera, Jusepe (1591-1652).

Born in Játiva near Valencia in 1591. Nothing is known of his activity in Spain, although he probably studied under Francisco Ribalta in Valencia. By 1616 he was established in Naples, having gone there via Parma, Padua and Rome. He worked under the patronage of the Duke of Osuna, then Viceroy of Naples, and of subsequent Viceroys.

Chiefly influenced by the works of Caravaggio (d. 1610) and his school. His first works to reach Spain were the « Crucifixion » and four other pictures sent there by the Duke of Osuna about 1616. From this date a large number of his works came to Spain, chiefly to Seville, where they had considerable influence. 1626 he was made a member of the Academy of St. Luke in Rome. 1625 he was visited in Naples by the Spanish biographer Jusepe Martínez and in 1630 by Velázquez. 1644 he was made a Knight of Christ by the Pope. Died in Naples in 1652.

Rizi, Fray Juan Andrés (1600-1681).

Born in Madrid in 1600, the son of the Bolognese artist Antonio Rizi, who went to Spain in 1585. Studied in Madrid under Maino. 1627 he entered a Benedictine monastery. 1640 he was appointed drawing master to Prince Baltasar Carlos. 1653 he executed a series of paintings for the monastery of « la Cogolla ». In 1662 he went to Italy where he entered the monastery of Montecassino; died there in 1681.

Rodrigo de Osona, the Younger (op. 1496(?)-1513).

The author of the «Adoration of the Kings» (National Gallery, London), signed « lo fil de mestre Rodrigo » (the son of Master Rodrigo); he can very probably be identified as the son of Rodrigo de Osona, an artist working in Valencia from 1476-1484 (?). The son also appears to be the Rodrigo de Osona referred to in documents of 1505-1513 in connection with work in Valencia Cathedral. Father and son probably collaborated in many works. The altarpiece for the chapel of St. Dionysius, Valencia Cathedral, ascribed to the son for stylistic reasons, was probably executed in 1496, the year in which the chapel is recorded to have been redecorated.

Roelas, Juan de las (1558/60-1625).

Born in 1558 or 1560, in Seville; in 1598-1602 he was in Valladolid where he helped in the decoration of the sepulchral monument to Philip II in 1598 (no longer extant). 1603 he was chaplain in Olivares (near Seville). 1616 he was royal chaplain in Madrid; in 1617 he applied unsuccessfully to be made court painter to Philip III. He returned to Seville where he painted for churches and monasteries. Died in Olivares in 1625.

Sánchez Coello, Alonso (1531/32-1588).

Born in 1531-32 in Benifairón (Valencia), of Portuguese parents. Studied in Lisbon and Flanders. From 1557 active at the Spanish court in Valladolid and was a favourite of Philip II. His personal acquaintance with Anthonis Mor is established by a letter from Cardinal Granvella (1583) who states that they were in his house together for several years. Set the style for court portraiture in Spain after Mor; he also painted altarpieces under the influence of Italian mannerism. Died in Madrid in 1588.

Sarabia, José de (1608 (?)-1669).

Born in Seville in 1608 (?). Probably studied under Augustín del Castillo and Zurbarán. He worked in Seville and Cordova; died in Cordova in 1669. Very few of his works are known; these are in the museum and churches of Cordova.

Serra, Jaime and Pedro (Jaime, op. 1361-1375; Pedro, op. 1363-1399).

Jaime first documented in 1361 when he received payment for a painting for the queen of Peter IV of Aragon. Died after 1375, before 1395.

Pedro is documented as collaborator of Jaime from 1363-1370; died after 1399.

The brothers Serra produced a large number of composite altar-pieces for churches in Aragon. Their work is very similar and they seem to have had a fairly extensive workshop. They popularized the theme of the Virgin and Child surrounded by angels and of the Virgin of Humility.

Theotocopoulos (Domenikos), El Greco (1541-1614).

Born in 1541 near Candia, Crete. He is undoubtedly the young Cretan, pupil of Titian, whom Giulio Clovio mentions in a letter in 1570 as having just arrived in Rome. 1572 probably left Rome to return to Venice. His works executed in Italy show the influence of Titian, Tintoretto and Jacopo Bassano.

1577 established in Toledo; the motives for his coming to Spain are unknown. His first known work in Spain is the altar for Santo Domingo el Antiguo, Toledo (1577). 1580 commissioned by Philip II to paint the « St. Maurice and the Theban Legion » for the Escorial. The picture did not please the king and Greco concentrated his activity in Toledo, where he formed an atelier and developed his own peculiar style, producing a very large number of works for churches and religious houses.

In 1586 the « Burial of Count Orgáz » was painted for the church of Santo Tomé, Toledo. He was in close contact with the most illustrious savants of his time and painted a number of portraits of them. Remained in Toledo until his death in 1614.

Tristán, Luis (c. 1586-1624).

Born about 1586. 1603-1606 he figures as a witness in various documents relating to El Greco in Toledo, and was in all probability a pupil of El Greco. According to Jusepe Martínez he went to Italy and there came under the influence of Ribera. 1613 he made a contract for paintings in the monastery of La Sisla, near Toledo (now lost). From this date he was active in Toledo; he executed a large number of altar-pieces for churches in the province of Toledo; the most important is that of the parish church of Yepes, executed in 1616. Died in Toledo in 1624.

Valdés Leal, Juan de (1622-1690).

Born in Seville in 1622. Spent his youth in Cordova where he probably studied painting under Antonio del Castillo. By 1657 he was working in Seville. He there formed, together with Murillo, an Academy of Painting of which he was president. He probably went to Madrid in 1674; died in Seville in 1690.

Vargas, Luis de (1502-1568).

Born in Seville in 1502. Probably studied in Italy and in 1551 was back in Seville. He was greatly influenced by the Roman mannerists whose style he introduced into Seville. The altar-piece of the « Genealogy of Christ » (*la Gamba*) was painted about 1551-3. Died in Seville in 1568.

Velázquez y Silva, Diego (1599-1660).

Born in Seville in 1599, he first studied painting under Francisco Herrera. 1612 he entered the studio of Francisco Pacheco and stayed until 1617 when he was made master painter. 1618 he married the daughter of Pacheco. 1622 he made his first journey to court, where he was made court painter to Philip IV. 1628 Rubens visited Madrid and was in close contact with Velázquez. 1629 he went to Italy visiting Parma, Rome and Venice, returning to Madrid in 1631. 1634 he was made assistant to the Master of the Robes and in this year he executed a series of large official portraits and also the « Surrender of Breda » for the decoration of the Salón de Reinos in the Buen Retiro. 1649 he went again to Italy to buy works of art for Philip IV. In Rome he painted the portrait of Pope Innocent X. He returned to Madrid in 1651. Next year he was made royal usher and in 1658 a knight of Santiago. Died in Madrid in 1660.

Zurbaran, Francisco (1598-post 1664).

Born in Fuente de Cantos (Badajoz) in 1598. 1614 apprenticed to Pedro Diáz de Villanueva in Seville. He also probably studied there under Juan de la Roelas. Circa 1625 he went to Llerena, but was recalled to Seville and asked to take up his permanent residence there.

1638 he signs himself «pintor del rey» (painter to the king). He was principally employed to work for religious houses in and near Andalusia; his most important series of paintings is that executed for the Jeronymite monastery of Guadalupe (1638-39). 1658 he was in Madrid and figured as a witness in the application of Velázquez to membership of the Order of Santiago. 1664, the last date in which he is documented, he was in Madrid.

BIBLIOGRAPHY

GENERAL WORKS

V. CARDUCHO : « Diálogos de la Pintura », Madrid, 1633. Second ed., 1865.

F. PACHECO : « Arte de la Pintura », Seville, 1649, second ed., Madrid, 1866.

J. MARTINEZ : « Discursos practicables del nobilísimo arte de la pintura » (1675 ?), Madrid, 1866.

A. A. PALOMINO de CASTRO Y VELASCO : « El museo pictórico y escala óptica », Madrid, 1715-24.

A. PONZ : « Viaje por España », Madrid, 1772, etc.

R. CUMBERLAND : « Anecdotes of eminent painters in Spain », London, 1782.

J. A. CEÁN BERMÚDEZ : « Diccionario histórico de los más ilustres profesores de las bellas artes en España », Madrid, 1800.

El conde de la VIÑAZA : « Adiciones al diccionario... de Juan Augustín Ceán Bermúdez », Madrid, 1894.

L. VIARDOT : « Notices sur les principaux peintres de l'Espagne », Paris, 1839.

Sir W. STIRLING-MAXWELL : « Annals of the artists of Spain », London, 1848.

J. PASSAVANT : « Die christliche Kunst in Spanien », Leipzig, 1853, Spanish ed., Seville, 1877.

M. R. ZARCO DEL VALLE : « Documentos inéditos para la historia de las bellas artes en España », Madrid, 1870.

C. BLANC : « Histoire des peintres : Ecole espagnole », Paris, 1880.

P. de MADRAZO : « Viaje artístico de tres siglos por las colecciones de cuadros de los reyes de España », Barcelona, 1884.

P. LEFORT : « La peinture espagnole », Paris, 1893.

C. G. HARTLEY : A record of Spanish painting », London, 1904.

E. BERTAUX & P. PARIS : « L'art en Espagne », In André Michel, « Histoire de l'art depuis les premiers temps chrétiens jusqu'à nos jours », Paris, 1905, etc.

C. JUSTI : « Miscellaneen aus drei Jahrhunderten spanischen Kunstlebens », Berlin, 1908.

E. BERTAUX : « Etudes d'histoire et d'art », Paris, 1910.

C. H. CAFFIN : « The story of Spanish painting », New York, 1910.

J. PIJOÁN : « Historia del arte », Barcelona, 1914-1916. English ed., New York, 1927.

A. de BERUETE Y MORET : « Spanish painting », London, Paris, New York, 1921.

A. L. MAYER : « Geschichte der spanischen Malerei », second ed., Leipzig, 1922. Spanish ed., Madrid, 1928.

V. von LOGA : « Die Malerei in Spanien », Berlin, 1923.

A. L. MAYER : « La pintura española » (Manuales Labor), Barcelona, 1926, second ed. 1929.

H. KEHRER : « Spanische Kunst », Munich, 1926.

P. PARIS : « La peinture espagnole », Paris, 1929.

C. R. POST : « A history of Spanish painting » (Harvard University Press), Cambridge, Mass., 1930. (In progress; six volumes published).

F. J. SÁNCHEZ CANTÓN : « Fuentes literarias para la historia del arte español ». (In progress; three volumes published). Madrid, 1933.

E. LAFUENTE FERRARI : « Breve historia de la pintura española » (Misiones de Arte), second ed., Madrid, 1936.

G. ROUCHÈS : « La peinture espagnole. Le moyen âge », Paris, 1928 (?)

A. L. MAYER : « El estilo románico en España », Madrid, 1931.

W. W. S. COOK : « Romanesque panel painting in Catalonia ». Dissertation for the degree of Doctor of Philosophy, Harvard University Library, 1923.

G. RICHERT : « Mittelalterliche Malerei in Spanien, Katalanische Wand- und Tafelmalereien », Berlin, 1925.

C. H. KUHN : « Romanesque mural painting in Catalonia » (Harvard University Press), Cambridge, Mass., 1930.

J. GUDIOL Y CUNILL : « La pintura mig-eval catalana. Els primitius ». Part I « La pintura mural , Barcelona, 1928. Part II « La pintura sobre fusta », Barcelona, 1929.

SANPERE Y MIQUEL : « La pintura mig-eval catalana. Els trescentistes », vol. I, Barcelona, 1924.

J. GUDIOL Y CUNILL : « La pintura mig-eval catalana. Els trescentistes », vol. II, Barcelona, 1924.

S. SANPERE Y MIQUEL : « Los cuatrocentistas catalanes : historia de la pintura en Cataluña en el siglo XV », Barcelona, 1906.

A. L. MAYER : « El estilo gótico en España », Madrid, 1929.

E. TORMO Y MONZÓ : « Desarrollo de la pintura española del siglo XVI » (Varios estudios de artes y letras), Madrid, 1902.

E. TORMO Y MONZÓ : « Los pintores de Felipe II », Madrid, 1924.

Fr. J. ZARCO CUEVAS : « Pintores españoles en San Lorenzo el Real del Escorial » (1566-1613), Madrid, 1931-1932.

F. J. SÁNCHEZ Y CANTÓN :« Los pintores de cámara de los reyes de España », Madrid, 1916.

E. MÂLE : « L'art religieux après le concile de Trente », Paris, 1932.

E. LAFUENTE FERRARI : « La pintura del siglo XVII en España » (« El Realismo en la pintura del siglo XVII »; Historia del arte labor, XII), Barcelona, 1935.

A. de BERUETE Y MORET : « Historia de la pintura española del siglo XIX », Madrid, 1926.

M. OSSORIO Y BERNARD : « Galeria biográfica de artistas españoles del siglo XIX ». Madrid, 1883-1884.

A. de BERUETE Y MORET : « The School of Madrid », London, 1909.

N. SENTENACH : « La pintura en Madrid », Madrid, 1907.

El barón de ALCAHALÍ : « Diccionario biográfico de artistas valencianos ». Valencia, 1897.

J. SANCHIS Y SIVERA : « Pinturas medievales en Valencia », Barcelona, 1916.

M. GONZÁLEZ MARTÍ : « Los grandes maestros del Renacimiento », Valencia (Chapters on Juanes, Ribalta, Ribera).

N. SENTENACH : « La pintura en Sevilla », Seville, 1885, English ed., London, 1911.

J. GESTOSO Y PÉREZ : « Ensayo de un diccionario de los artífices que florecieron en Sevilla », Seville, 1899-1900.

A. L. MAYER : « Die Sevillaner Malerschule : Beiträge zu ihrer Geschichte », Leipzig, 1911.

« Documentos para la historia del arte en Andalucia » (Universidad de Sevilla, Laboratorio de arte), Seville, 1927. (In progress).

R. RAMÍREZ de ARELLANO : « Diccionario biográfico de artistas de la provincia de Córdoba », Madrid, 1893.

A. BAQUERO ALMANSA : « Catálogo de los profesores de las bellas artes murcianos », Murcia, 1913.

A. FURIÓ : « Diccionario histórico de los ilustres profesores de las bellas artes en Mallorca », Palma, 1839.

MONOGRAPHS

BERMEJO

E. TORMO Y MONZÓ : « Bartolomé Bermejo », Madrid, 1926.

BERRUGUETE

J. LAFORA : « De Pedro Berruguete ». In « Arte español », No 4, 1926.

BORASSA

J. GUDIOL Y CUNILL : « El pintor Luis Borrassá », Barcelona, 1926.

CANO

M. GÓMEZ MORENO : « Alonso Cano » (in « Cosas granadinas de arte y arqueología »), Granada,

CARREÑO

D. BERJANO ESCOBAR : « El pintor D. Juan Carreño de Miranda », Madrid, 1924.

COELLO

C. PÉREZ BUSTAMENTE : « Claudio Coello; Noticias biográficas desconocidas » in « Boletin de la Sociedad Española de Excursiones », 1918.

ESPINOSA

L. TRAMOYERES BLASCO : « El pintor Jerónimo Jacinto de Espinosa, en el Museo de Valencia », Valencia, 1916.

FERNÁNDEZ

D. ANGULO ÍÑIGUEZ : « Alejo Fernández... », in « Archivo Español de Arte y Arqueología », 1930.

GOYA

L. MATHERON : « Goya », Paris, 1858. Spanish ed. 1890.

P. G. BRUNET : « Étude sur Francisco Goya, sa vie et ses travaux », Paris, 1865.

C. YRIARTE : « Goya », Paris, 1867.

F. ZAPATER Y GÓMEZ : « Goya, noticias biográficas », Saragossa, 1868.

G. CRUZADA VILLAAMIL : « Los tapices de Goya », Madrid, 1870.

P. LEFORT : « Francisco Goya », Paris, 1877.

El Conde de la VINAZA : « Goya, su tiempo, su vida, sus obras », Madrid, 1887.

C. ARAUJO SÁNCHEZ : « Goya », Madrid, 1895.

W. ROTHENSTEIN : « Goya », London, 1900.

P. LAFOND : « Goya » (Étude extraite de la « Revue de l'art ancien et moderne »), Paris, 1902.

E. TORMO Y MONZÓ : « Las pinturas de Goya y su clasificación cronológica » (in « Varios estudios de artes y letras », Madrid, 1902.

R. OERTEL : « Francisco Goya ». (« Künstler-Monografien. Knackfuss), Bielefeld and Leipzig, 1907.

A. F. CALVERT : « Goya, an account of his life and works », London, 1908.

H. STOKES : « Francisco Goya », London, 1914.

A. de BERUETE Y MORET : « Goya », Madrid, 1917-19. Vol. I « Pintor de Retratos », English ed., London, 1922. Vol. II « Composiciones y figuras ». Vol. III « Grabador ».

V. LOGA : « Francisco de Goya », second ed., Berlin, 1921.

A. L. MAYER : « Francisco de Goya », Munich, 1923. English ed., London and Toronto, 1924. Spanish ed., Barcelona, 1925.

CALLEJA : « Goya, cuadros, dibujos, biografía, epistolario », Madrid, 1924.

SALCADO Y RUIZ : « La época de Goya », Madrid, 1924.

MADRID, Museo del Prado : « Catálogo ilustrado de la Exposición de pinturas de Goya... », Madrid, April-May, 1928.

F. J. SÁNCHEZ CANTÓN : « Goya » (Maîtres d'autrefois), Paris, 1930.

E. HARRIS : « The followers of Goya ». Thesis for the degree of Doctor of Philosophy, University of London Library, 1933 (MS.).

GRECO

A. F. CALVERT & C. G. HARTLEY : « El Greco », London, New York, 1909.

F. de B. SAN ROMÁN : « El Greco en Toledo », Madrid, 1910.

P. LAFOND : « Le Greco », Paris, 1913.

A. L. MAYER : « El Greco », Berlin, 1913.

H. KEHRER : « Die Kunst des Greco », Munich, 1914.

A. L. MAYER : « El Greco. Kritisches Verzeichnis », Munich, 1926.

M. B. COSSÍO : « El Greco », Madrid, 1928.

J. F. WILLUMSEN : « La jeunesse du peintre El Greco », Paris, 1927.

F. de B. SAN ROMÁN : « De la vida del Greco », Madrid, 1927.

E. K. WATERHOUSE : «El Greco's Italian Period». (Art Studies, 1930, I).

A. L. MAYER : « El Greco », Berlin, 1931.

M. LEGENDRE & A. HARTMANN : « El Greco, Paris, London, 1937.

HERRERA

J. S. THACHER : « The paintings of Francisco de Herrera, the Elder ». Thesis for the degree of Doctor of Philosophy, University of London Library, 1936 (MS.).

HUGUET

B. ROWLAND, Jr. : « Jaume Huguet : a study of late gothic painting in Catalonia » (Harvard University Press), Cambridge, Mass., 1932.

JACOMART

E. TORMO Y MONZÓ : « Jacomart y el arte hispano-flamenco cuatrocentista », Madrid, 1913.

JUANES

VILANOVA Y PIZCUETA : « Biografía de Juan de Juanes, su vida y obras », Valencia, 1884.

MAINO

E. HARRIS : « Aportaciones para el estudio de Juan Bautista Manio », in « Revista Española de Arte », December, 1935.

MORALES

E. TORMO Y MONZÓ : « El divino Morales », Barcelona, 1917.

D. BERJANO ESCOBAR : « El divino Morales », Madrid, 1921.

J. de HINOJOS : «El divino Morales. Ensayo íntimo», Cáceres, 1926.

MURILLO

F. M. TUBINO : « Murillo », Seville, 1864.

C. B. CURTIS : « Velázquez and Murillo. A descriptive catalogue », London, New York, 1883.

L. ALFONSO : « Murillo. El hombre. El artista. Las obras », Barcelona, 1886.

P. LEFORT : « Murillo et ses élèves », Paris, 1892.

P. LAFOND : « Murillo, biographie critique », Paris, 1902.

C. JUSTI : « Murillo », Leipzig, 1892. Second ed. 1904.

A. F. CALVERT : « Murillo », London, New York, 1907.

A. de VALENCINA : « Murillo y los Capuchinos », Seville, 1908.

A. L. MAYER : « Murillo » (Klassiker der Kunst), Stuttgart and Berlin, 1913.

S. MONTOTO Y SEDA : « Bartolomé Esteban Murillo. Estudio biográfico crítico », Seville, 1923.

S. MONTOTO Y SEDA : « Murillo », Barcelona, 1932.

ORRENTE

L. TRAMOYERES Y BLASCO : « El pintor Pedro Orrente... », in « Archivo de Arte valenciano », September, 1916.

PACHECO

J. M. ASENSIO Y TOLEDO : « Francisco Pacheco; sus obras artísticas », Seville, 1867.

F. RODRÍGUEZ MARÍN : « Francisco Pacheco, maestro de Velázquez », Madrid, 1923.

RIBALTA

L. TRAMOYERES Y BLASCO : « Los pintores Francisco y Juan Ribalta », in « Archivo de Arte valenciano », July-December 1917.

RIBERA

P. LAFOND : « Ribera et Zurbarán. Biographies critiques », Paris, 1909.

A. L. MAYER : « Jusepe de Ribera », Leipzig, 1908. Second ed. 1923.

G. PILLEMENT : « Ribera » (« Maîtres de l'art ancien »), Paris, 1929.

RIZI

TORMO, GUSI Y LAFUENTE : « La vida y la obra de Fr. Juan Ricci », Madrid, 1930.

ROELAS

A. L. MAYER : « Juan de Roelas » in « Monatshefte für Kunstwissenschaft », 1911.

D. ANGULO ÍNIGUEZ : « Juan de las Roelas, aportaciones para su estudio », in « Archivo Español, de Arte y Arqueología », January-April, 1925.

TRISTÁN

P. QUINTERO : « Luis Tristán », in « Boletín de la Sociedad Española de Excursiones », 1909.

F. de B. SAN ROMAN : « Noticias nuevas para la biografía del pintor Luis Tristán », Toledo, 1924.

VALDÉS LEAL

C. LÓPEZ MARTÍNEZ : « Valdés Leal y sus discípulos », Seville, 1907.

A. de BERUETE : « Valdés Leal. Estudio crítico », Madrid, 1911.

J. GESTOSO Y PÉREZ : « Biografía del pintor sevillano Juan de Valdés Leal », Seville, 1917.

C. LÓPEZ MARTÍNEZ : « Valdés Leal », Seville, 1922.

P. LAFOND : « Juan de Valdés Leal », Paris.

VELÁZQUEZ

C. JUSTI : «Diego Velázquez und sein Jahrhundert», Bonn, 1868. English ed., London, 1889.

C. B. CURTIS : « Velázquez and Murillo. A descriptive catalogue », London, New York, 1883.

Sir W. STIRLING-MAXWELL : « Velázquez and his works », London, 1885.

G. CRUZADA VILLAAMIL : « Anales de la vida y las obras de Diego de Silva Velázquez », Madrid, 1885.

P. LEFORT : « Velázquez », Paris, 1888.

R. A. M. STEVENSON : « The art of Velázquez », London, 1895.

Sir WALTER ARMSTRONG : « Art and life of Velazquez », 1896.

J. O. PICÓN : « Vida y obras de Don Diego Velázquez », Madrid, 1899.

R. A. M. STEVENSON : « Velazquez », London, 1906.

A. de BERUETE Y MORET : « Velázquez », Paris, 1898. London, 1906. Berlin, 1909

P. LAFOND : « Diego Velazquez ». Paris, 1906.

A. F. CALVERT & C. G. HARTLEY : «Velazquez», London, New York, 1908.

W. GENSEL : « Velazquez » (Klassiker der Kunst), second ed., Stuttgart and Leipzig, 1908.

E. TORMO Y MONZÓ : « Velázquez y el Salón de Reinos del Buen Retiro », Madrid, 1912.

A. L. MAYER : « Kleine Velazquez Studien », Munich, 1913.

J. MORENO VILLA : « Velázquez », Madrid, 1920.

A. de BERUETE Y MORET : « La paleta de Velázquez », Madrid, 1922.

A. L. MAYER : « Diego Velazquez », Berlin 1924.

J. ALLENDE-SALASAR : « Velázquez » (Klassiker der Kunst), Stuttgart, fourth ed., Berlin and Leipzig, 1926 (?)

A. L. MAYER : « Velazquez. A catalogue raisonné of the pictures and drawings », London, 1936.

ZURBARÁN

E. TORMO Y MONZÓ : « El monasterio de Guadalupe y los cuadros de Zurbarán », Madrid, 1905.

P. LAFOND : « Ribera et Zurbarán. Biographies critiques », Paris, 1909.

J. CASCALES Y MUÑOZ : «Francisco de Zurbarán», Madrid, Seville, 1911. Second ed. 1931. English ed., New York, 1918.

H. KEHRER : « Francisco de Zurbarán », Munich, 1918.

SPANISH ART PERIODICALS

« Anuari de l'Institut d'estudis catalans », Barcelona, 1907, etc.

« Archivo de Arte Valenciano », Valencia.

« Archivo español de arte y archeología » (« Centro de Estudios historicos»), Madrid, 1925, etc.

« El Arte en España », Madrid, 1862, etc.

« Arte Español. Revista de la Sociedad de Amigos del Arte », Madrid, 1912, etc.

« Boletín de la Sociedad Castellana de Excursiones », Valladolid.

« Boletín de la Sociedad Española de Excursiones », Madrid, 1893, etc.

« Illustració Catalana », Barcelona, 1903, etc.

« Museum. Revista mensual de Arte español antiguo y moderno », Barcelona, 1911, etc.

« Revista de Archivos, Bibliotecas y Museos », Madrid, 1871, etc.

« Revista crítica Hispano-Americana », Madrid, 1915, etc.

« Revista española de Arte. Publicación de la Sociedad Española de Amigos del Arte », Madrid, 1931, etc.

« Vell i Nou », Barcelona.

PRINTED IN BELGIUM.

1

Lazarus at the Gate of the Rich Man.
Circa 1123.
Detail of wall-painting from San Clemente de Tahull.
Museum, Barcelona. — Photo Arxiu Mas.

Lazarus at the Gate of the Rich Man.
Circa [illegible]
Detail of wall-painting from San Clemente de Tahull.
Museum, Barcelona. Photo Arxiu Mas

16798

THE LIBRARY
COLBY JUNIOR COLLEGE
NEW LONDON, N. H

2

Virgin and Child.
Wall-painting from the apse of the church of Sorpe.
Second half of the XIIth century.
Museum, Barcelona. — Photo Arch. Phot. d'Art et d'Histoire.

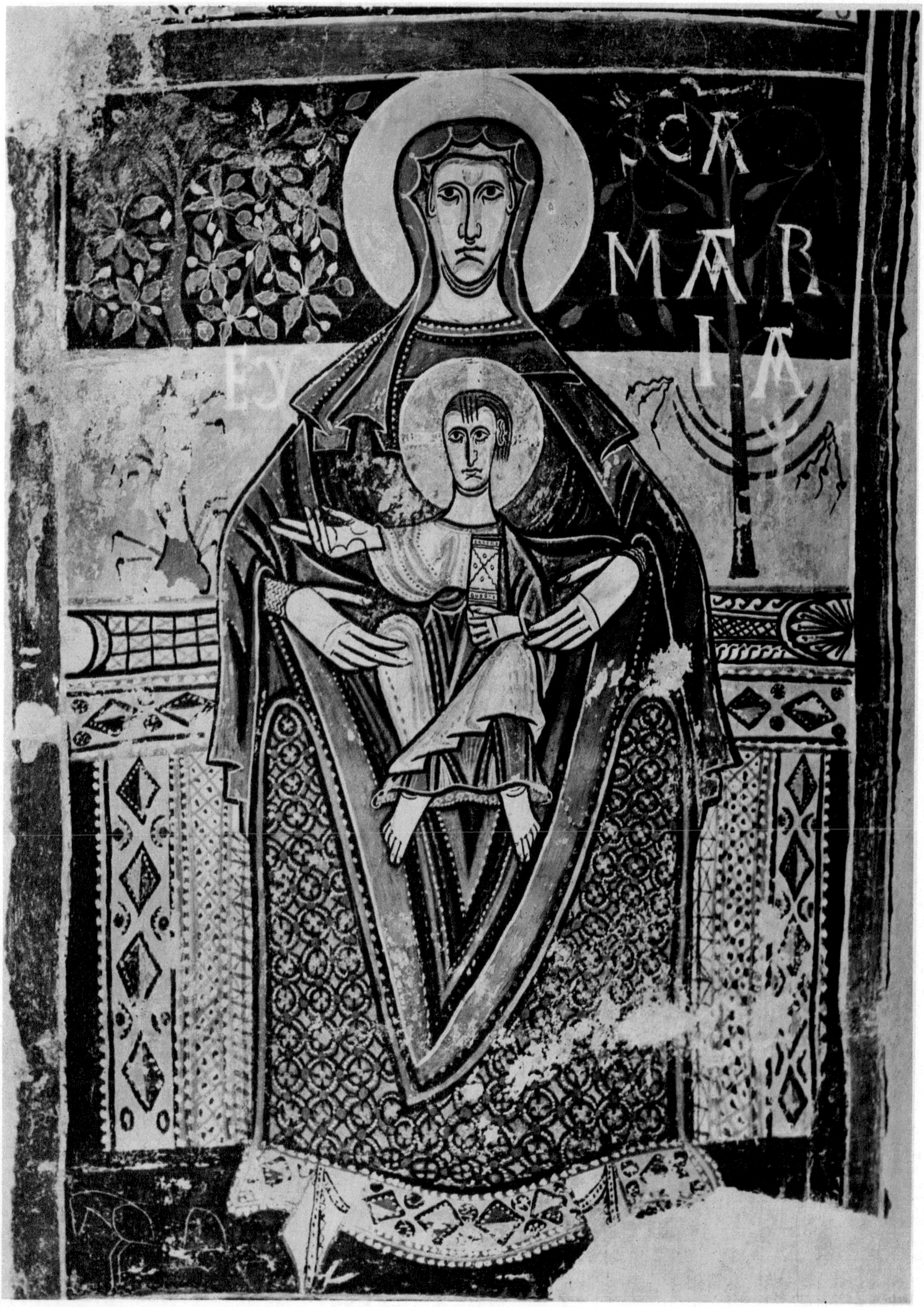
SCA
MAR
IA

3

A Prophet.
Wall-painting from the apse of S. Pedro del Burgal.
Circa 1200.
Museum, Barcelona. — Photo Arch. Phot. d'Art et d'Histoire.

4

SS. Julitta and Quiricus.
Altar frontal.
Second half of the XIIth century.
Museum, Barcelona. — Photo Arch. Phot. d'Art et d'Histoire.

5

FERRER BASSA

The Virgin and Child with Angel (Detail).
1346. — 1,01 m. by 1,27 m.
Wall-painting in the Chapel of San Miguel.
Franciscan Convent of Pedralbes. Barcelona.
Photo Arxiu Mas.

6

FERRER BASSA

The Nativity.
1346. — 1,27 m. by 1,49 m.
Wall-painting in the Chapel of San Miguel,
Franciscan Convent of Pedralbes, Barcelona.
Photo Arxiu Mas.

6

7

FERRER BASSA

Mourning over the dead Christ.
1346. — 1,30 m. by 1,21 m.
Wall-painting in the Chapel of San Miguel,
Franciscan Convent of Pedralbes, Barcelona.
Photo Arxiu Mas.

8

JAIME SERRA (?)

The Virgin of Humility.
Circa 1373. — Panel.
Collection Roman Vicente, Saragossa.
Photo Arxiu Mas.

9

PEDRO SERRA

The Transfiguration.

1394.

Section of the retable of the Pentecost.

Cathedral of Manresa. — Photo Arxiu Mas.

10

LUIS BORASSÁ

The Presentation of the Veronica to Abgar (Detail). 1412-1415.
Section of the retable of Santa Clara.
Episcopal Museum, Vich. — Photo Arxiu Mas.

10

LUIS BORRASSÁ
The Presentation of the Veronica to Abgar (?) (c. 1412-1415).
Section of the retable of Santa Clara.
Episcopal Museum, Vich. — Photo Arxiu Mas.

11

CATALAN SCHOOL

The Nursing Madona.
Section of the retable of Cervera.
Museum, Barcelona. — Photo Arch. Phot. d'Art et d'Histoire.

II

CATALAN SCHOOL

The Nursing Madonna.

Section of the retable of Cervera.

Museum, Barcelona. — Photo Arch. Phot. d'Art et d'Histoire.

12

ANDRES MARZÁL DE SAX

The Incredulity of St. Thomas.
Circa 1400.
Cathedral of Valencia. — Photo Arxiu Mas.

13

VALENCIAN SCHOOL

St. Michael.
First half of the XVth century.
Panel, 1,79 m. by 0,91 m.
National Gallery of Scotland, Edinburgh. — Photo Annan.

14

VALENCIAN SCHOOL

Retable of St. George.
Victoria and Albert Museum, London.
Photo Victoria and Albert Museum.

15

VALENCIAN SCHOOL

St. George assisting at the Baptism of the King, Queen and Princess.
Section of the retable of St. George.
Victoria and Albert Museum, London.
Photo Victoria and Albert Museum.

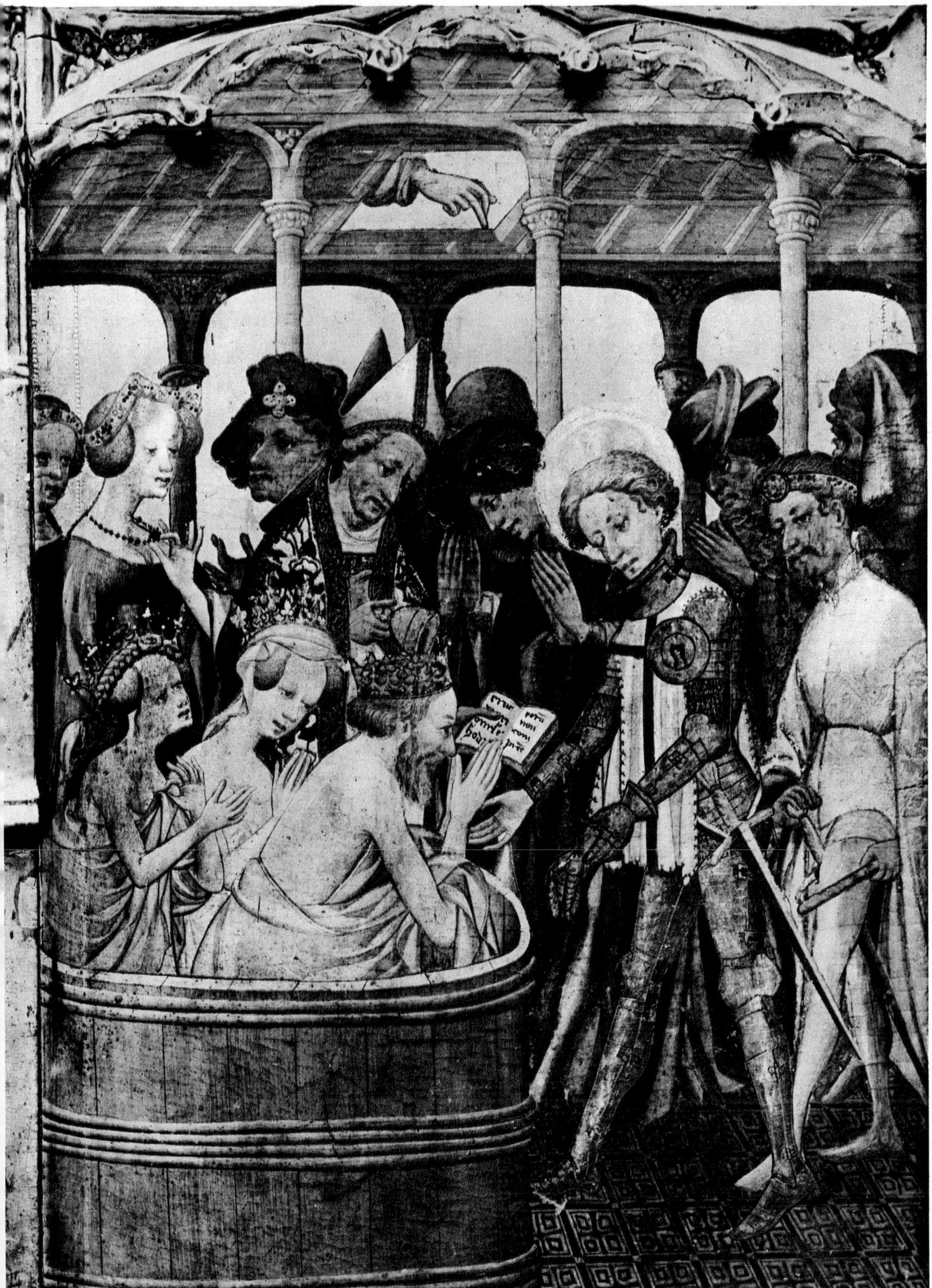

16

LUIS DALMAU

The Virgin of the Councillors (Detail).
1445 (signed and dated).
Museum, Barcelona. — Photo Arxiu Mas.

16

LUIS DALMAU

The Virgin of the Councillors (Detail).
1445 (Signed and dated).
[illegible], Barcelona. — Photo Arxiu Mas.

17

JACOMART

St. Martin and the Beggar.
Section of the retable of St. Martin.
1447 or 1457 (dated). — 0,62 m. by 0,62 m.
Diocesan Museum, Segorbe. — Photo Arxiu Mas.

18

MAÎTRE ALFONSO

The Martyrdom of St. Cucufas.
1473. — Panel.
Museum, Barcelona. — Photo Arxiu Mas.

19

PEDRO DE CORDOBA

The Annunciation.

1475 (signed and dated).

Cathedral of Cordova. — Photo Arxiu Mas.

20

BARTOLOMÉ BERMEJO

The Virgin with the dead Christ.
1490. — Panel, 1,89 m. by 1,75 m.
Cathedral of Barcelona. — Photo Arxiu Mas.

21

FERNANDO CALLEGO

Head of St. John (Detail of the Crucifixion).
Collection Weibel, Madrid.
Photo Arxiu Mas.

22

RODRIGO DE OSUNA THE YOUNGER

St. Dionysius (Detail).
Circa 1496.
Cathedral of Valencia. — Photo Arxiu Mas.

23

PEDRO BERRUGUETE

The Apparition of the Virgin to a Domenican Community.
1,26 m. by 0,78 m.
Prado, Madrid. — Photo Anderson.

24

ALEJO FERNANDEZ

The Virgin as Patron of Merchant Ships.
National Palace, Madrid. — Photo Arxiu Mas.

25

LUIS DE VARGAS

The Genealogy of Christ, « La Gamba » (Detail).
1561 (signed and dated).
Cathedral of Seville. — Photo Arxiu Mas.

QVIS
QVO
ENIM

26

JUAN DE JUANES
The Assumption of the Virgin.
0,92 m. by 0,61 m.
Provincial Museum, Valencia. — Photo Arxiu Mas.

27

LUIS DE MORALES

The Virgin with the dead Christ.
Academy of San Fernando, Madrid. — Photo Anderson.

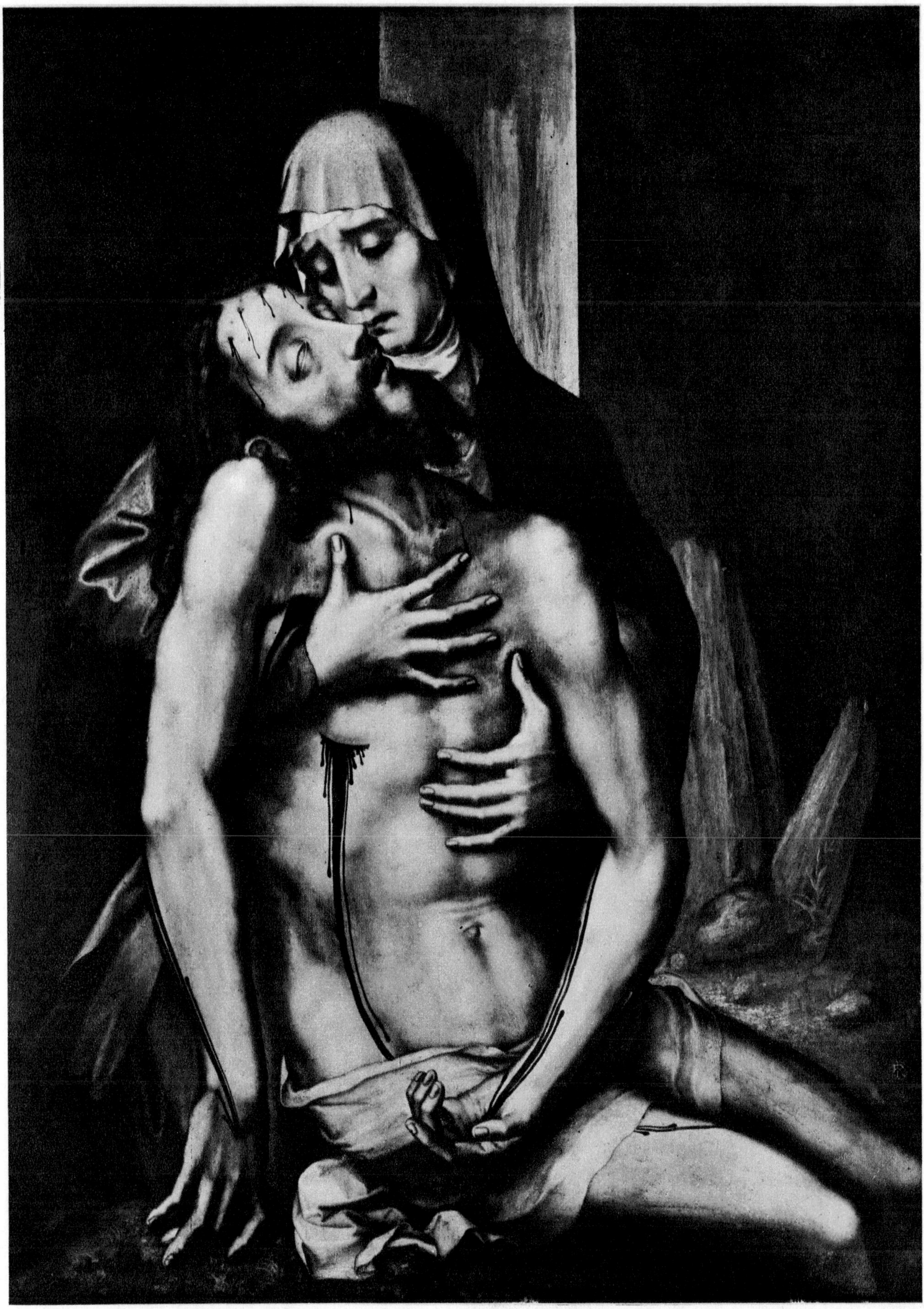

I

EL GRECO

St. Louis of France (or St. Ferdinand of Castile). Detail.
Circa 1586-1590. — Canvas, 1,17 m. by 0,95 m.
Musée du Louvre, Paris.

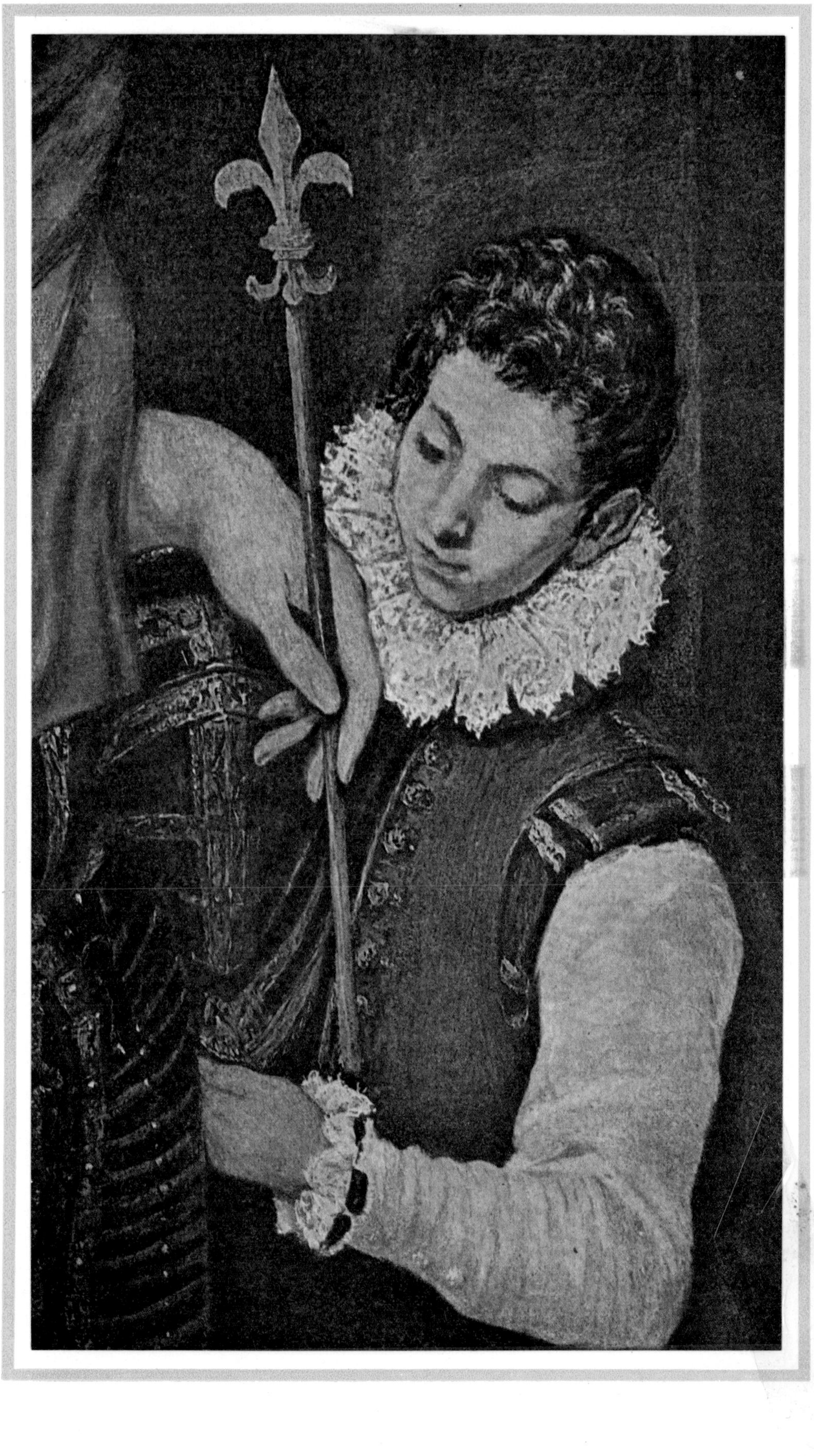

28

NAVARRETE (LE MUET)

The Burial of St. Lawrence.

1579.

Monastery of the Escorial. — Photo Moreno.

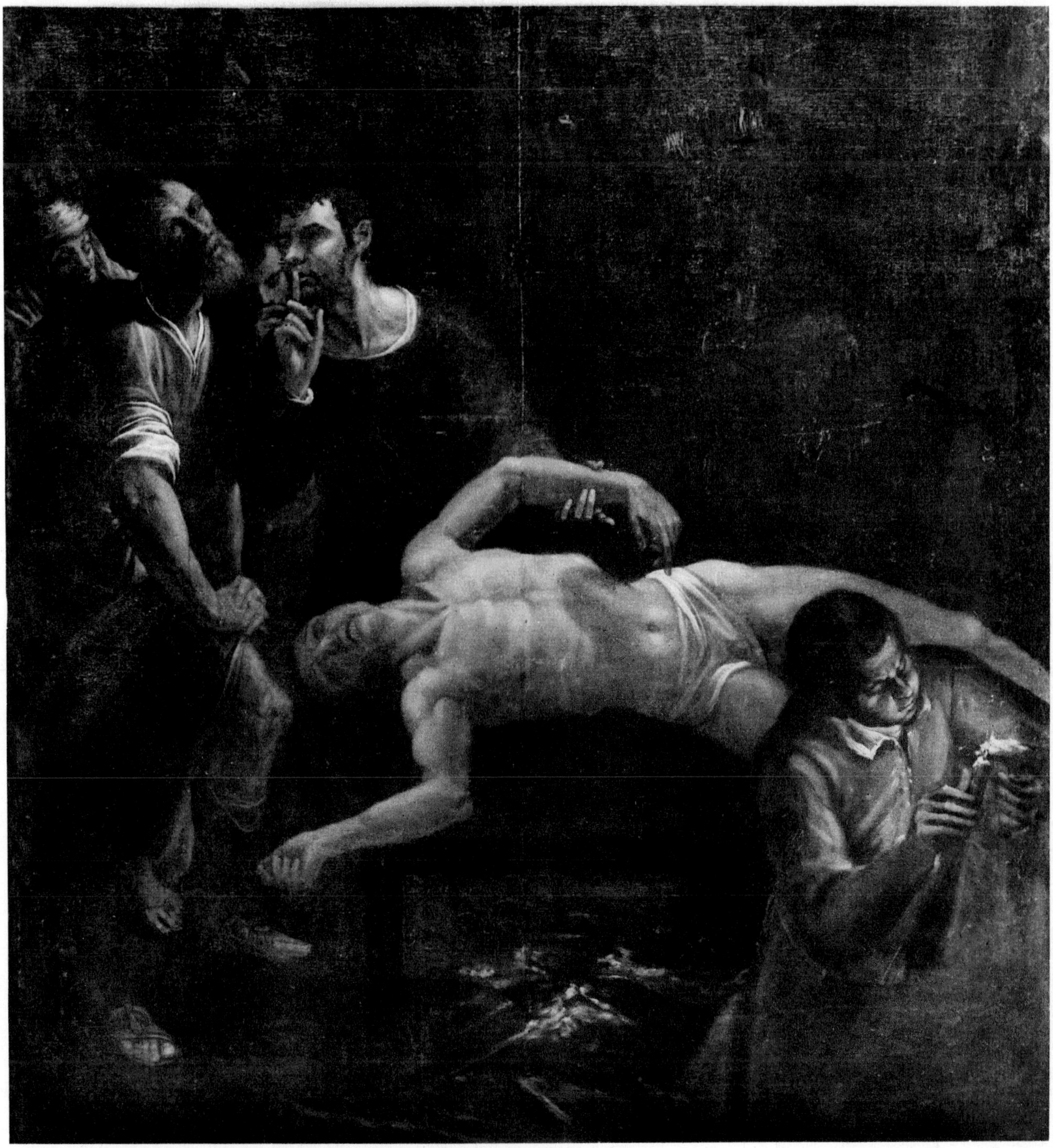

29

ALONSO SANCHEZ COELLO

Portrait of Anne of Austria, fourth wife of Philip II.
1571 (signed and dated). — 1,75 m. by 0,96 m.
Kunsthistorisches Museum, Vienna. — Photo Wolfrum.

ALONSO SANCHEZ COELLO

Portrait of the Infante Don Carlos.
Circa 1568. — 1,86 m. by 0,82 m.
Kunsthistorisches Museum, Vienna. — Photo Wolfrum.

30

JUAN PANTOJA DE LA CRUZ

Portrait of Fray Hernando de Roxas (Detail).
1595 (signed and dated).
Collection Duquesa de Espeja, Madrid.
Photo Moreno.

el V.º fr. her.do, de roxas
Conpañero, del p.e m.o,
fr. Al.o de orozco, y ad
ministradror, desta
obra

31

EL GRECO

Spanish Proverb (Detail).
0,67 m. by 0,88 m.
Collection Mark Oliver, London.
Photo courtesy of Mr. Mark Oliver.

32

EL GRECO

The Trinity (Detail).
1577. — 3,00 m. by 1,79 m.
Prado, Madrid. — Photo Arxiu Mas.

33

EL GRECO

The Martyrdom of St. Maurice (Detail).
1580-1584. — 4,44 m. by 3,02 m.
Monastery of the Escorial. — Photo Moreno.

34

EL GRECO

The Burial of Count Orgaz (Detail).
1586. — 4,80 m. by 3,60 m.
Church of Santo Tomé, Toledo. — Photo Anderson.

35

EL GRECO

The Burial of Count Orgaz.
(Detail : Angel with the soul of Count Orgaz).
1586. — 4,80 m. by 3,60 m.
Church of Santo Tomé, Toledo. — Photo Rodriguez.

36

EL GRECO

Portrait of Antonio Covarrubias (Detail).
1594-1600. — 0,66 m. by 0,52 m.
Museo del Greco, Toledo. — Photo Moreno.

II

EL GRECO

The Expulsion of the Moneylenders from the Temple. (Detail).
Canvas, 1,055 m. by 1,27 m.
National Gallery, London.

37

EL GRECO

The Assumption of the Virgin.
Circa 1613. — 3,23 m. by 1,67 m.
Museum of San Vicente, Toledo. — Photo Arxiu Mas.

38

LUIS TRISTAN

Portrait of a Man.

0,47 m. by 0,34 m.

Prado, Madrid. — Photo Moreno.

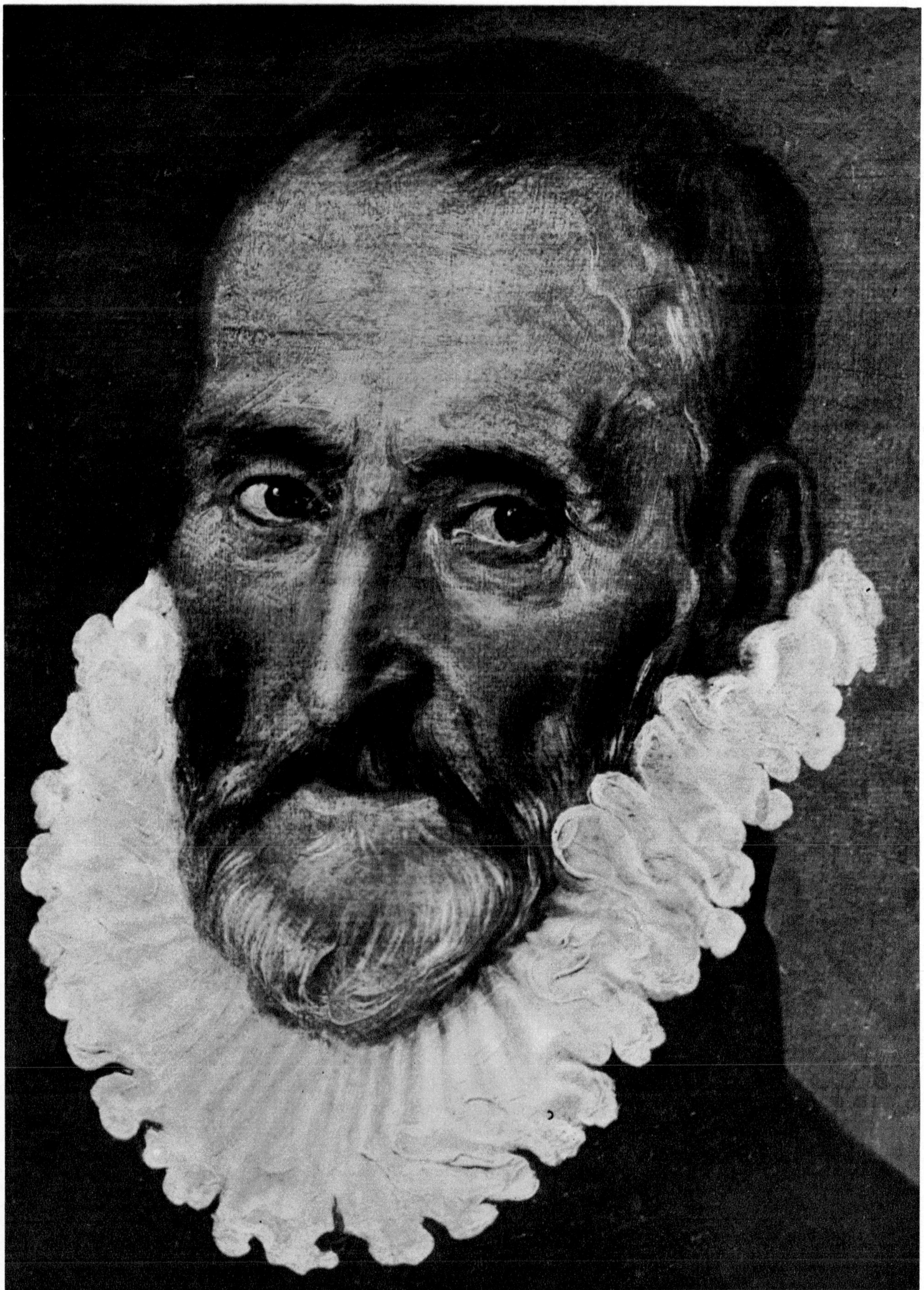

39

LUIS TRISTAN

The Trinity (Detail).
1624 (signed and dated). — 1,50 m. by 0,98 m.
Cathedral of Seville. — Photo Arxiu Mas.

40

JUAN BAUTISTA MAINO

The Adoration of the Shepherds.
1612. — 3,14 m. by 1,75 m.
Museum, Villanueva y Geltrú. — Photo Arxiu Mas.

41

JUAN BAUTISTA MAINO
Portrait of a Dominican Monk.
0,46 m. by 0,33 m.
Collection Percy Moore Turner, London.
Photo courtesy of Mr. P. M. Turner.

42

JUAN BAUTISTA MAINO

The Recovery of Bahía (Detail).
Circa 1634. — 3.09 m. by 3,81 m.
Prado, Madrid. — Photo Arxiu Mas.

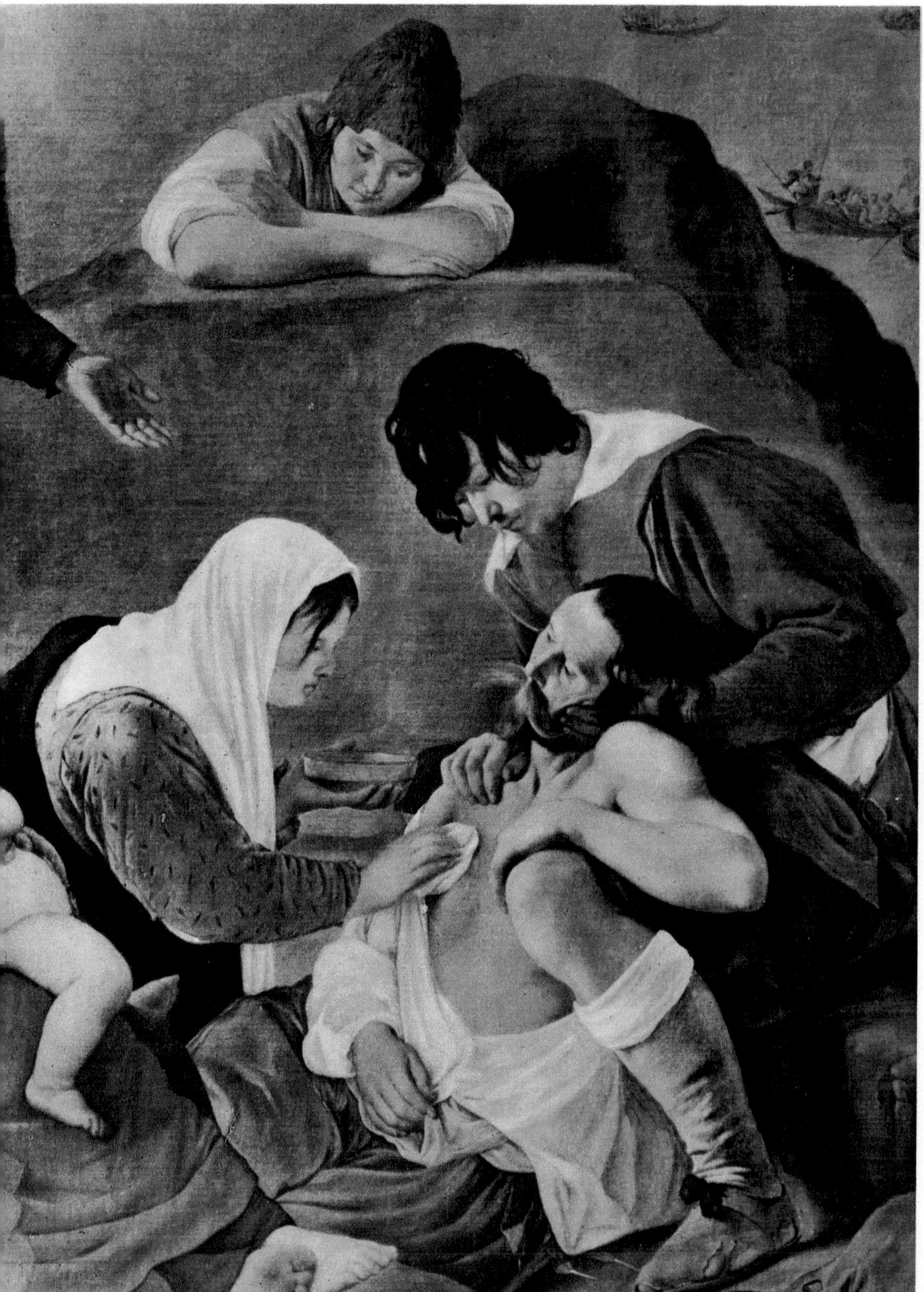

III

JUSEPE RIBERA

Apollo and Marsyas.
Signed and dated 1637. — Canvas, 2,00 m. by 2,45 m.
Musée des Beaux-Arts, Brussels.

43

PEDRO ORRENTE

Christ healing the Sick.
0,83 m. by 1,16 m.
Kunsthistorisches Museum, Vienna. — Photo Wolfrum.

44

PEDRO ORRENTE

The Apparition of St. Leocadia to St. Ildefonso (Detail).
Circa 1617.
Cathedral of Toledo. — Photo Arxiu Mas.

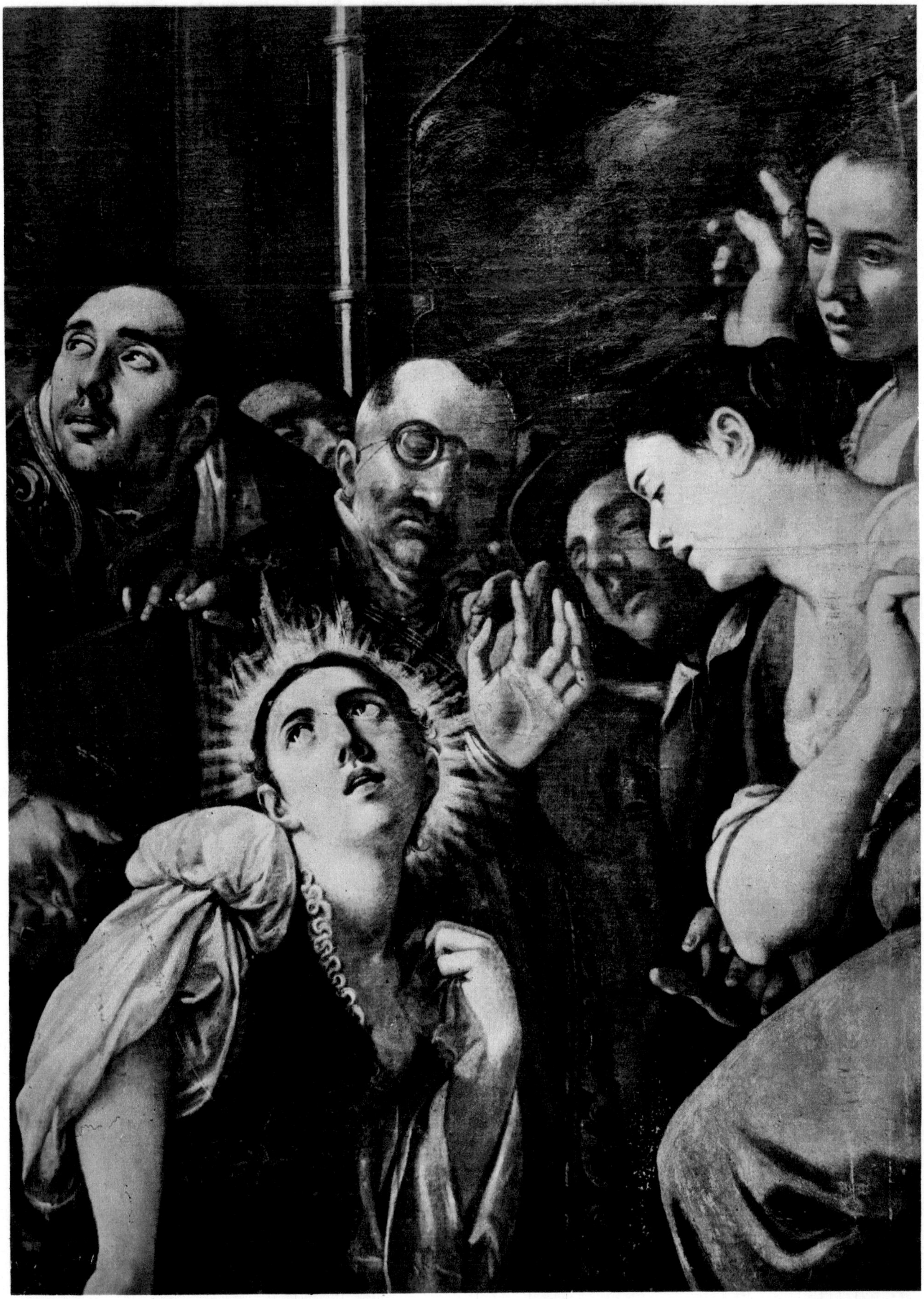

45

VICENTE CARDUCHO

The Vision of St. Francis.
1631 (signed and dated). — 2,46 m. by 1,73 m.
Museum, Budapest. — Photo Hanfstaengl.

46

FRANCISCO RIBALTA

Saint Francis embracing Christ on the Cross.
Circa 1620. — 2,30 m. by 1,70 m.
Provincial Museum, Valencia. — Photo Arxiu Mas.

I.N.R.I.

47

JUAN RIBALTA

Christ nailed to the Cross (Detail).
1628 (signed and dated). — 3,10 m. by 2,40 m.
Provincial Museum, Valencia. — Photo Arxiu Mas.

IESVS NAZARENVS REX IVDEORṼ

48

JUSEPE RIBERA

The Martyrdom of St. Bartholomew.
1630 (or 1639?) (signed and dated). — 2,34 m. by 2,34 m.
Prado, Madrid. — Photo Anderson.

49

JUSEPE RIBERA

The Trinity.
Circa 1636. — 2,26 m. by 1,81 m.
Prado, Madrid. — Photo Anderson.

50

JUSEPE RIBERA

St. Agnes (Detail).
1641 (signed and dated). — 2,02 m. by 1,52 m.
Museum, Dresden.

51

JUSEPE RIBERA

Communion of the Apostles (Detail).
1651 (signed and dated). — 4,00 m. by 4,00 m.
Church of the Certosa di San Martino, Naples.
Photo Anderson.

IV

JUSEPE RIBERA

The Club-Foot.

Signed and dated 1652. — Canvas, 1,64 m. by 0,92 m.

Musée du Louvre, Paris.

DA MIHI ELIMO
PROPTER
REM DEI

52

JUAN DE LAS ROELAS

The Virgin of « La Merced » with Saints of the Order.
Circa 1611.
Cathedral of Seville. — Photo Arxiu Mas.

53

JUAN DE LAS ROELAS

The Adoration of the Shepherds.
Circa 1624. — 2,35 m. by 1,17 m.
Church of La Merced, Sanlúcar de Barrameda.
Photo Arxiu Mas.

54

FRANCISCO HERRERA

St. Basil dictating his Doctrine.
2,50 m. by 1,95 m.
Musée du Louvre, Paris.
Photo Arch. Phot. d'Art et d'Histoire.

55

FRANCISCO PACHECO

The Immaculate Conception.
Cathedral of Seville. — Photo Arxiu Mas.

56

DIEGO VELÁZQUEZ

Portrait of Doña Gerónima de la Fuente (Detail).
1620 (signed and dated). — 2,00 m. by 1,28 m.
Convent of Santa Isabel de los Reyes, Toledo.

FRANCISCO PACHECO

Portrait of a Donor (Detail).
Panel, 0,36 m. by 0,60 m.
Provincial Museum, Seville. — Photo Arxiu Mas.

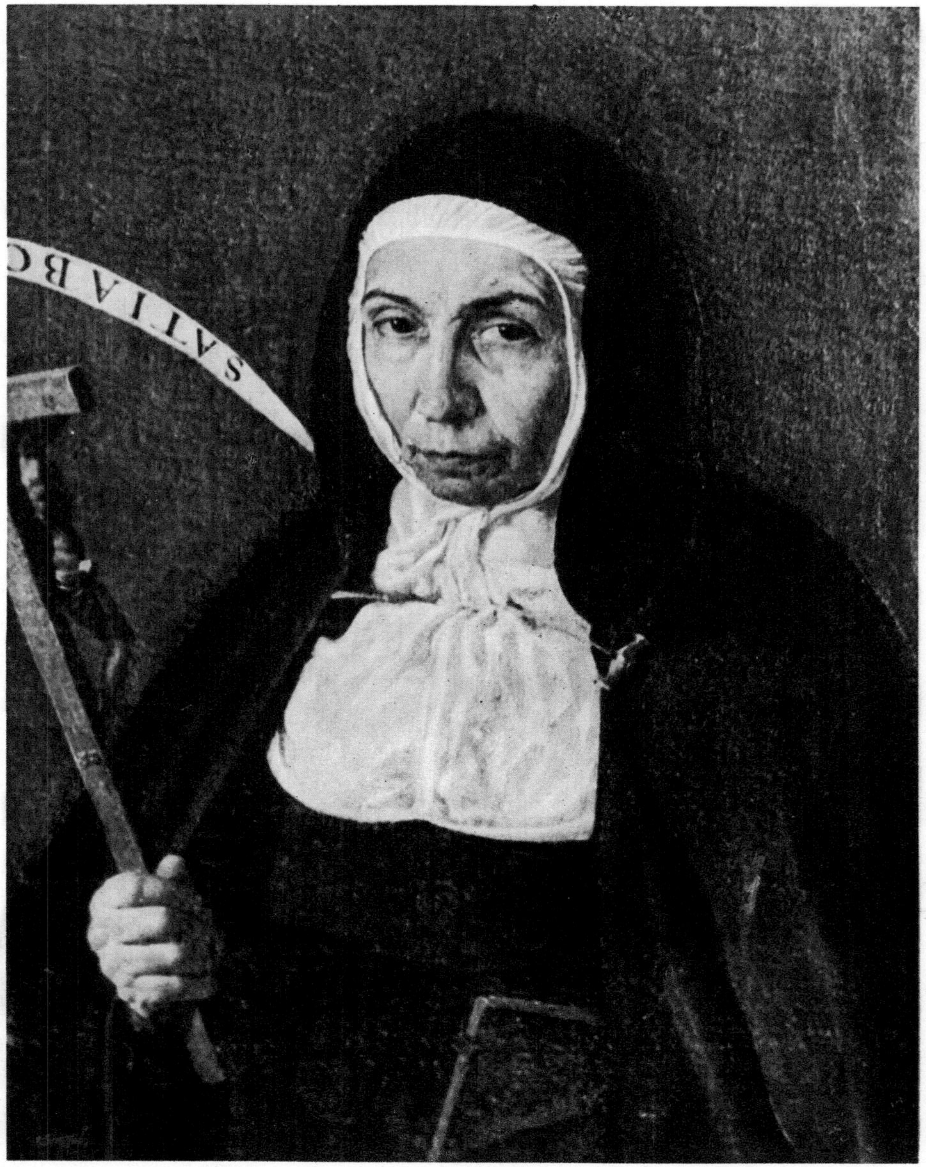
SATIAB

57

DIEGO VELÁZQUEZ

The Adoration of the Kings (Detail).
1619 (?) (dated). — 2,03 m. by 1,25 m.
Prado, Madrid. — Photo Anderson.

58

DIEGO VELÁZQUEZ

St. Ildefonso receiving a Chasuble from the Virgin.
Circa 1621. — 1,65 m. by 1,15 m.
Archbishop's Palace, Seville. — Photo Anderson.

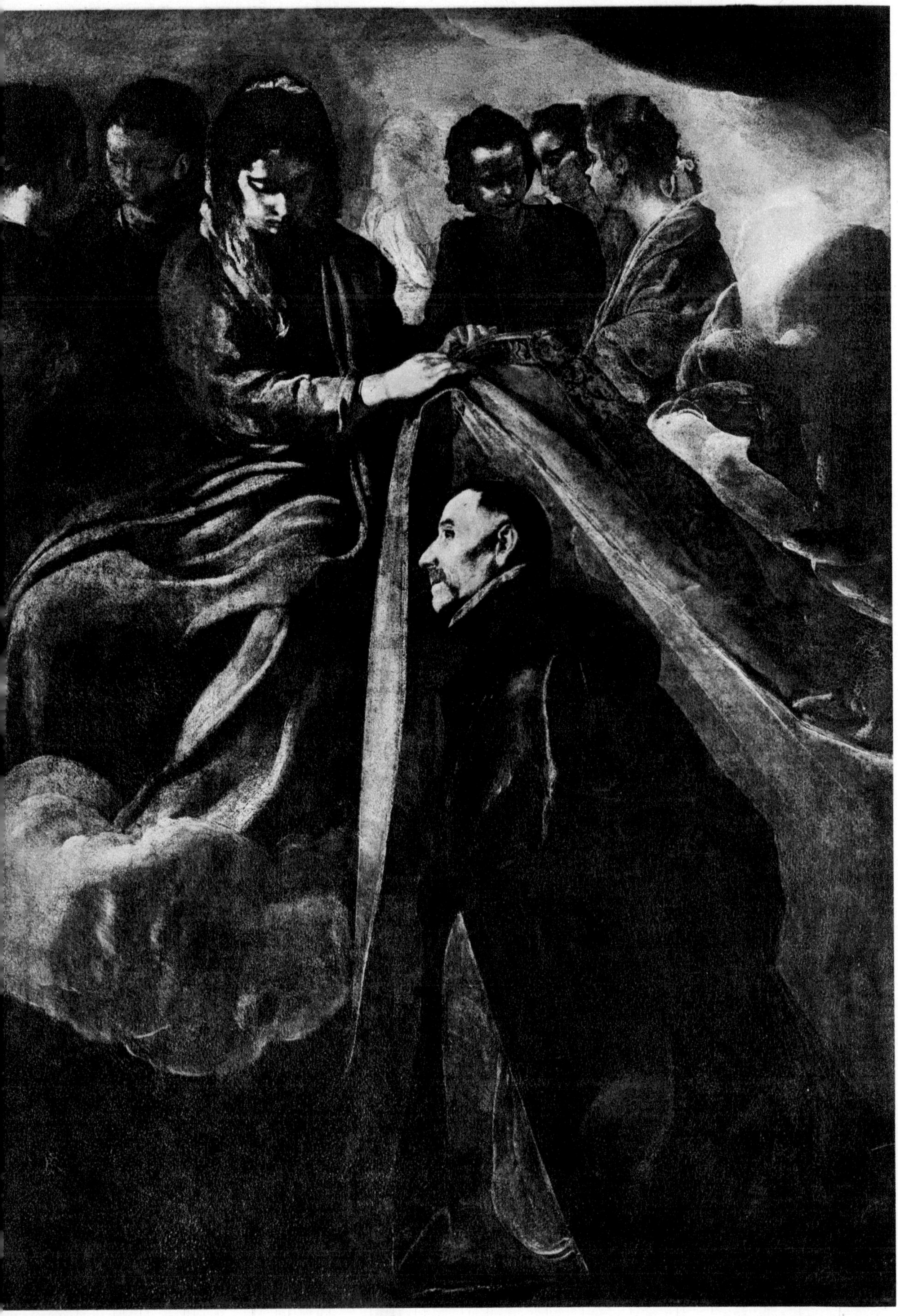

59

DIEGO VELÁZQUEZ
Philip IV (Detail).
Circa 1628. — 2,01 m. by 1,02 m.
Prado, Madrid. — Photo Moreno.

DIEGO VELÁZQUEZ
Philip IV (Detail).
Circa 1655-1660. — 0,69 m. by 0.56 m.
Prado, Madrid. — Photo Anderson.

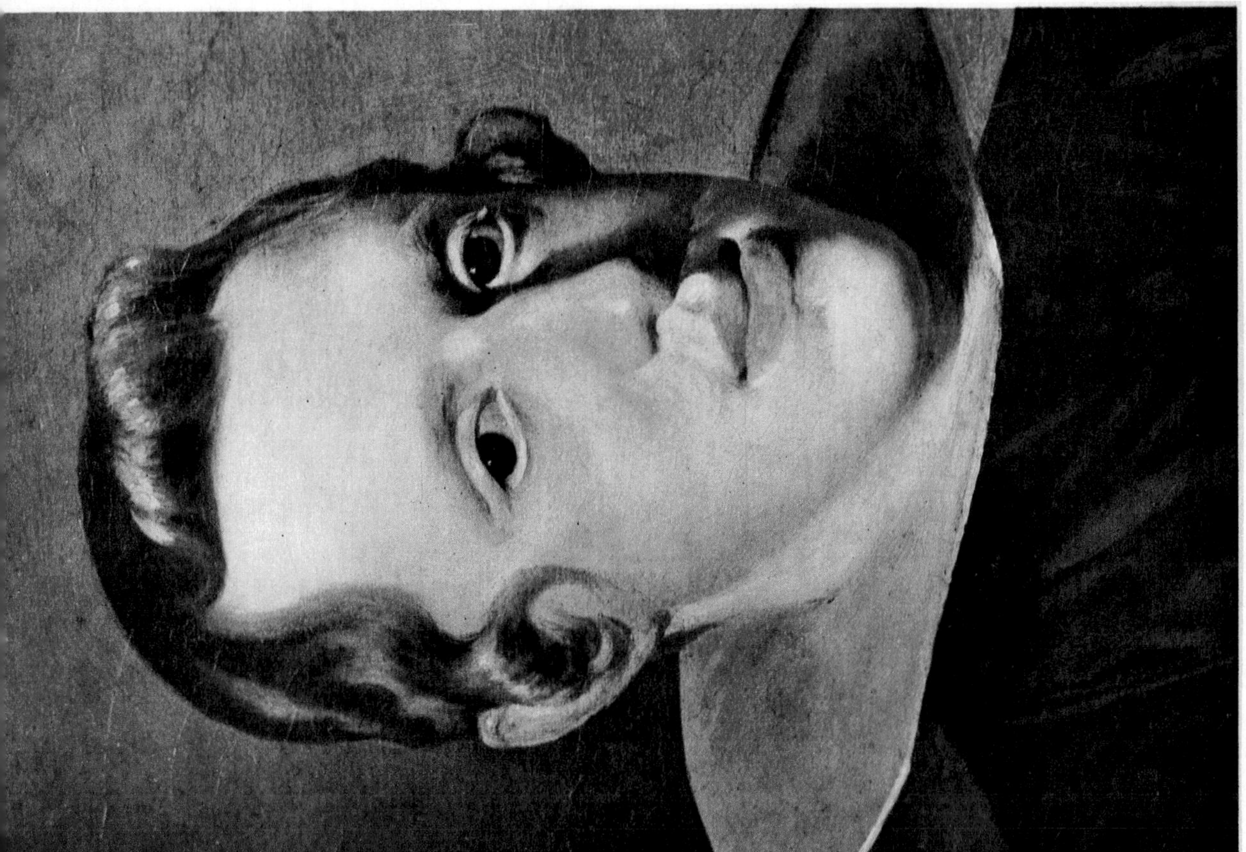

60

DIEGO VELÁZQUEZ

The Surrender of Breda (Detail).
Circa 1634. — 3,07 m. by 3,67 m.
Prado, Madrid. — Photo Anderson.

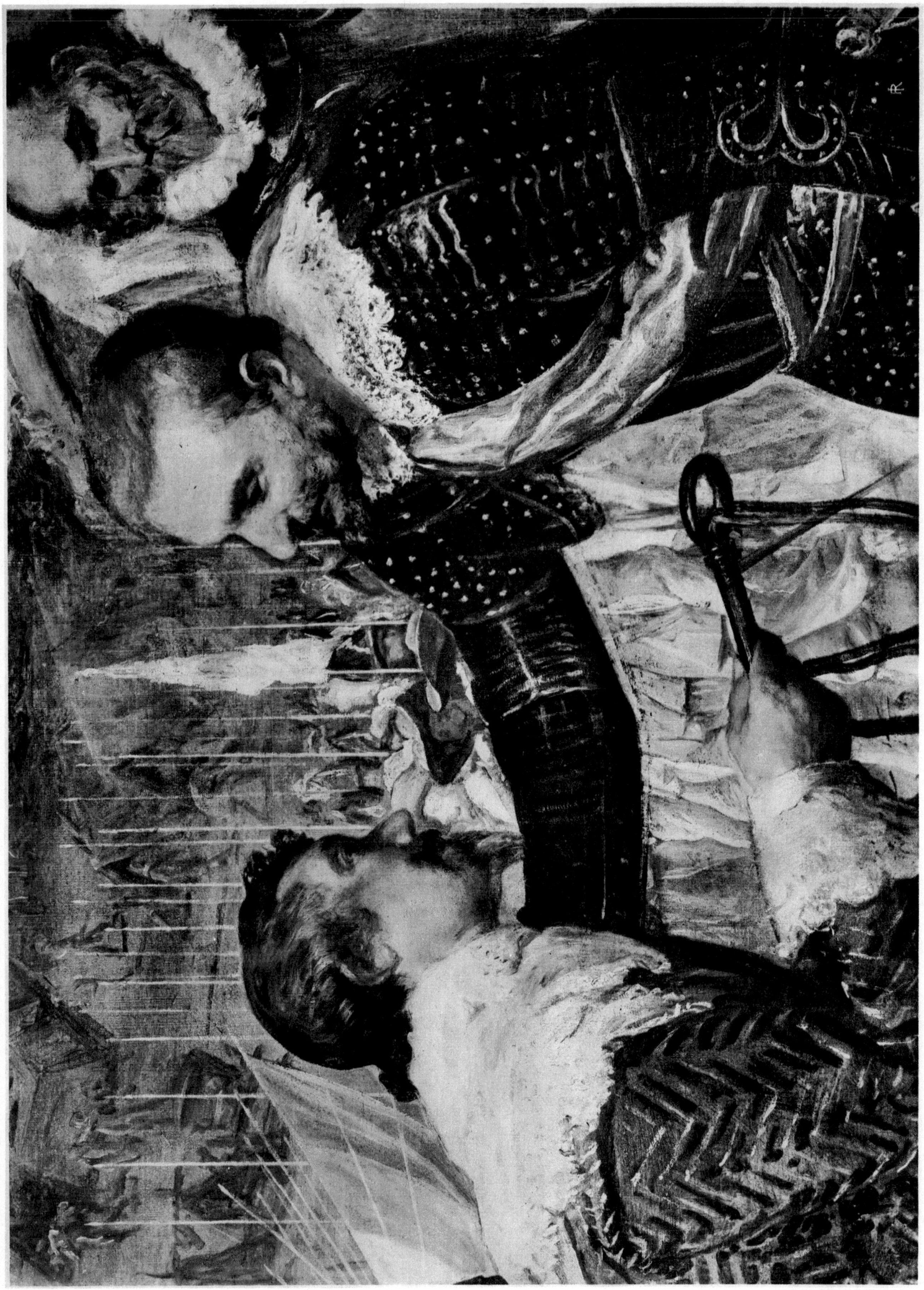

61

DIEGO VELÁZQUEZ
« El Niño de Vallecas » (Detail).
Circa 1646. — 1,07 m. by 0,83 m.
Prado, Madrid. — Photo Anderson.

DIEGO VELÁZQUEZ
Prince Baltasar Carlos (Detail).
1635-1636. — 1,91 m. by 1,03 m.
Prado, Madrid. — Photo Moreno.

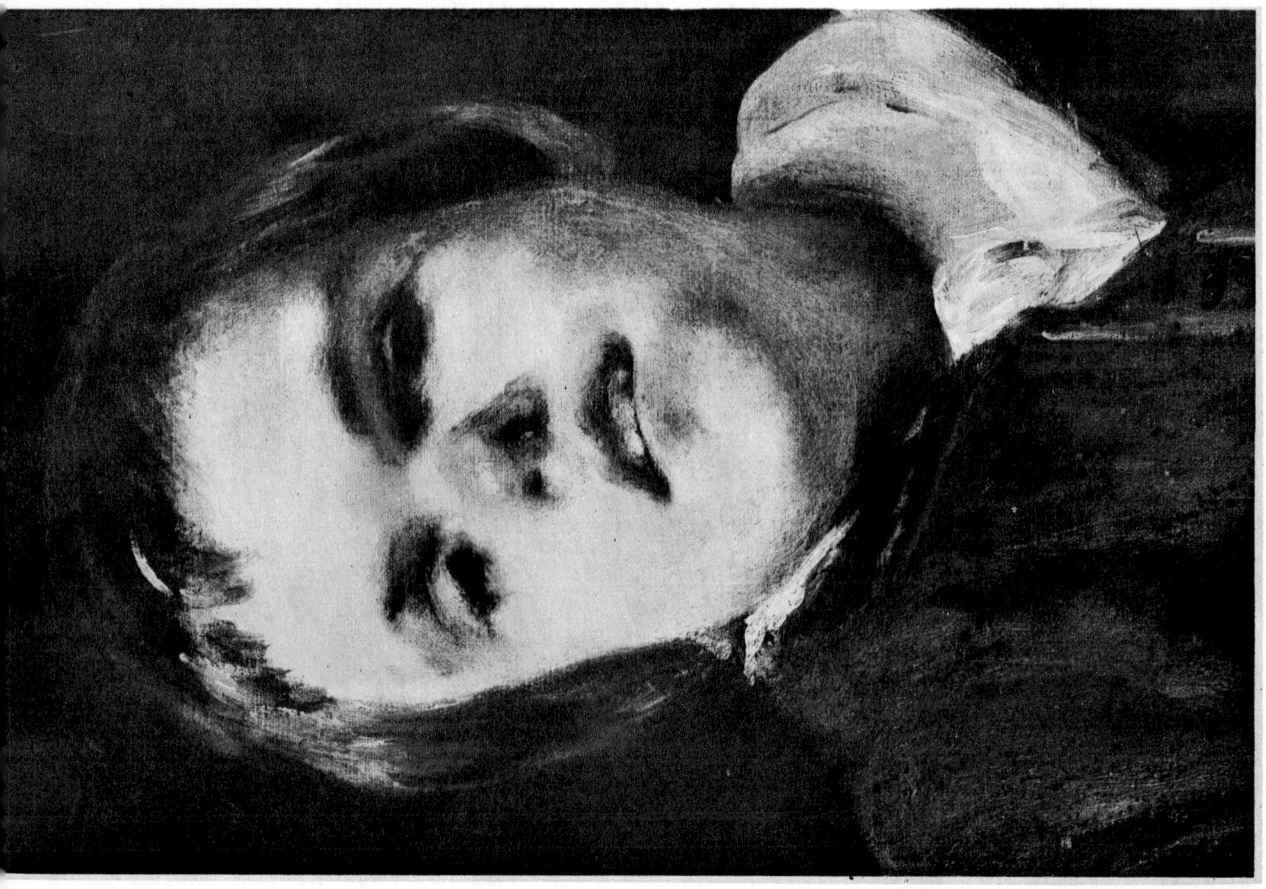

V

DIEGO VELÁZQUEZ

The Infanta Maria Teresa. (Detail).
Circa 1653. — Canvas, 1,27 m. by 0,89 m.
Kunsthistorisches Museum, Vienna.

62

FRANCISCO DE ZURBARÁN

St. Peter.
1633 (signed and dated).
Museum, Lisbon.

DIEGO VELÁZQUEZ

Aesop.
Circa 1639-1640. — 1,79 m. by 0,94 m.
Prado, Madrid. — Photo Anderson.

ÆSOPVS

63

FRANCISCO DE ZURBARÁN
The Tears of St. Peter (Detail).
1625.
Altar of St. Peter, Cathedral of Seville.
Photo Laboratorio de Arte, Seville.

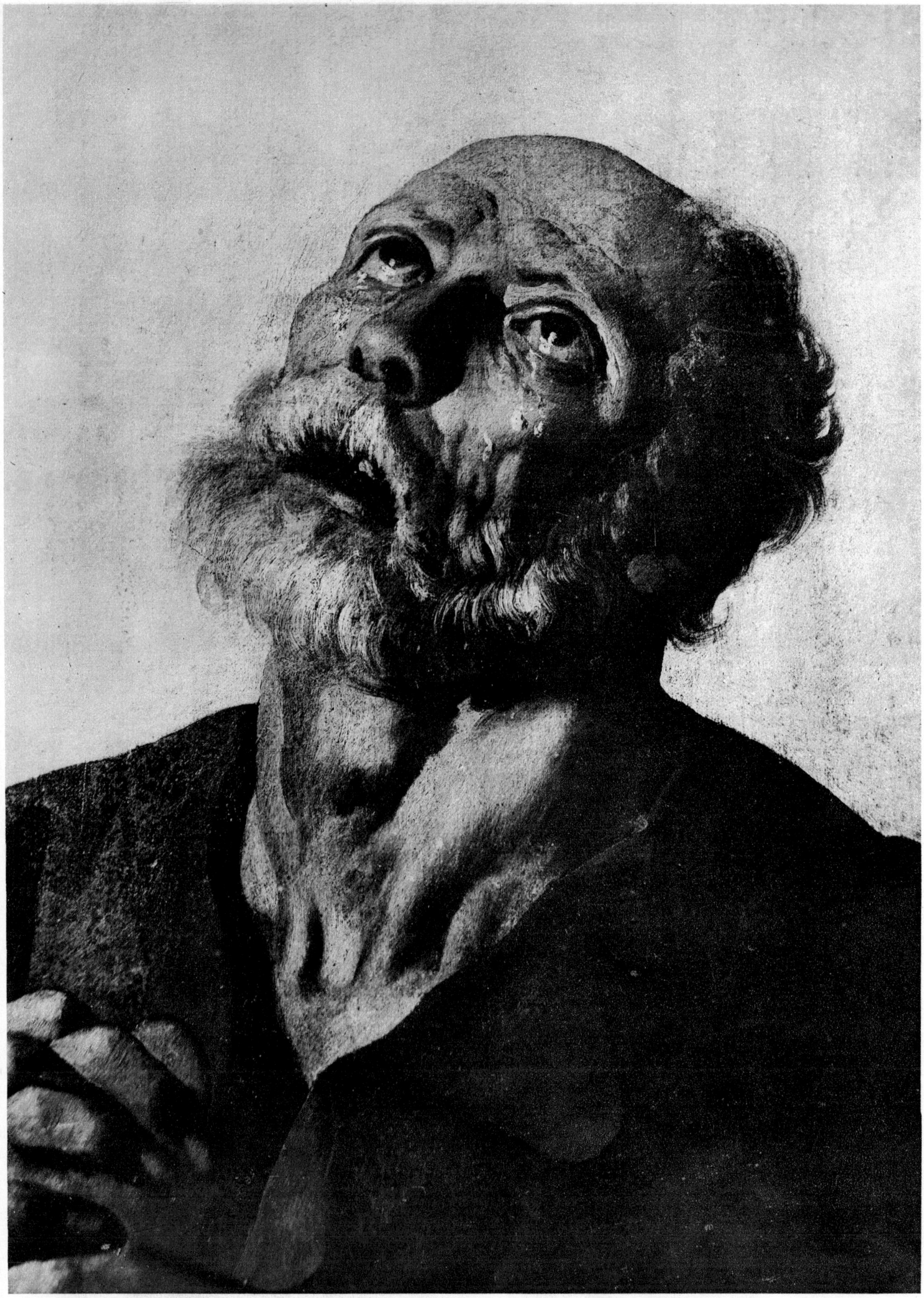

64

FRANCISCO DE ZURBARÁN

The Adoration of the Shepherds (Detail).
1638 (signed and dated). — 2,61 m. by 1,75 m.
Museum, Grenoble. — Photo Bulloz.

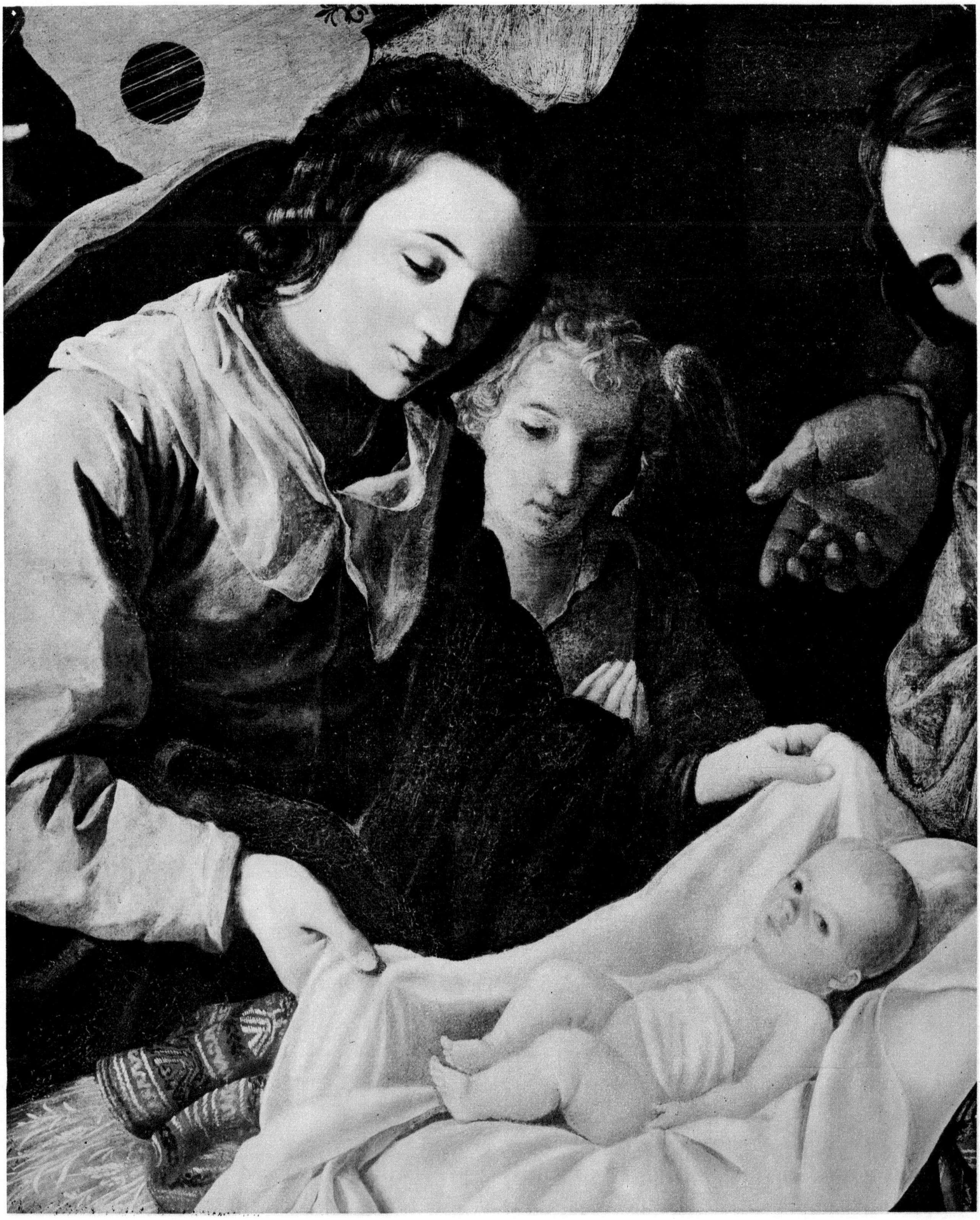

65

FRANCISCO DE ZURBARÁN

The Flagellation of St. Jerome.
1638-1639.
Monastery of Guadelupe. — Photo Arxiu Mas.

66

FRANCISCO DE ZURBARÁN

The Immaculate Conception.
1661 (signed and dated). — 1,36 m. by 1,02 m.
Museum, Budapest. — Photo Braun.

67

JOSÉ SARABIA

The Adoration of the Shepherds.
Provincial Museum, Cordova. — Photo Arxiu Mas.

67

JOSE SARABIA

The Adoration of the Shepherds

[illegible] Museum, [illegible] Photo [illegible] Mas

68

JERONIMO JACINTO ESPINOSA
The Vision of St. Ignatius Loyola.
1653.
Provincial Museum, Valencia. — Photo Arxiu Mas.

69

JUAN BAUTISTA DEL MAZO

Portrait of Queen Mariana of Austria.
1666 (signed and dated). — 1,95 m. by 1,44 m.
National Gallery, London. — Photo National Gallery.

MADRE

70

JUAN BAUTISTA DEL MAZO

The Artist's Family.

Circa 1655. — 1,50 m. by 1,72 m.

Kunsthistorisches Museum, Vienna. — Photo Wolfrum.

71

JUAN CARREÑO DE MIRANDA

Portrait of Eugenia Martínez Vallejo, « La Monstrua ».
1,65 m. by 1,07 m.
Prado, Madrid. — Photo Anderson.

72

JUAN CARREÑO DE MIRANDA
Portrait of Queen Mariana of Austria.
1,82 m. by 1,32 m.
Alte Pinakothek, Munich. — Photo Hanfstaengl.

73

JUAN RIZI

St. Benedict celebrating Mass.
Academy of San Fernando, Madrid.
Photo Anderson.

74

ALONSO CANO

The Vision of St. Anthony of Padua.
1,60 m. by 1,09 m.
Alte Pinakothek, Munich. — Photo Hanfstaengl.

75

ALONSO CANO

The Communion of the Virgin.
0,87 m. by 0,45 m.
Palazzo Bianco, Genoa. — Photo Alinari.

76

BARTOLOMÉ ESTEBAN MURILLO

The Charity of St. Diego of Alcalá.
1645. — 1,70 m. by 1,86 m.
Academy of San Fernando, Madrid. — Photo Anderson.

77

BARTOLOMÉ ESTEBAN MURILLO

St. Leander.

1655. — 1,88 m. by 1,86 m.

Cathedral of Seville. — Photo Arxiu Mas.

CREDITE
O GOTHI
CONSVBS
TANTIALEM
PATRI

78

BARTOLOMÉ ESTEBAN MURILLO

The Miracle of Moses striking the Rock (Detail).
1670-1674. — 3,35 m. by 5,50 m.
Hospital de la Caridad, Seville. — Photo Anderson.

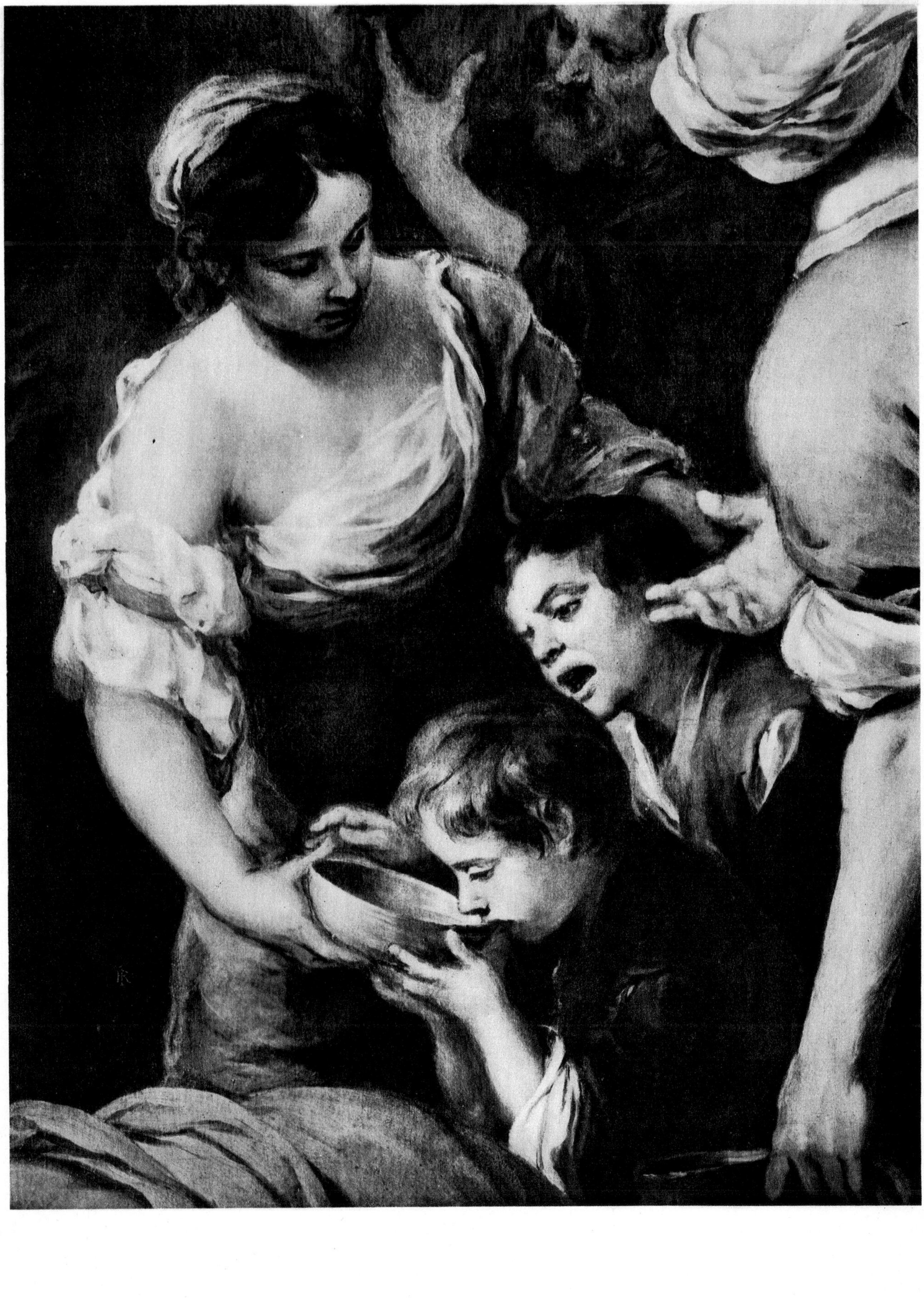

79

BARTOLOMÉ ESTEBAN MURILLO

Self-Portrait.
Circa 1675. — 1,19 m. by 1,07 m.
Collection of Earl Spencer, Althorp.
Photo courtesy of Earl Spencer.

Bart.^{us} Murillo seipsum depin
gens pro filiorum votis acpreci
bus explendis

80

BARTOLOMÉ ESTEBAN MURILLO

St. Francis embracing Christ on the Cross (Detail).
1674-1676. — 2,77 m. by 1,81 m.
Provincial Museum, Seville. — Photo Arxiu Mas.

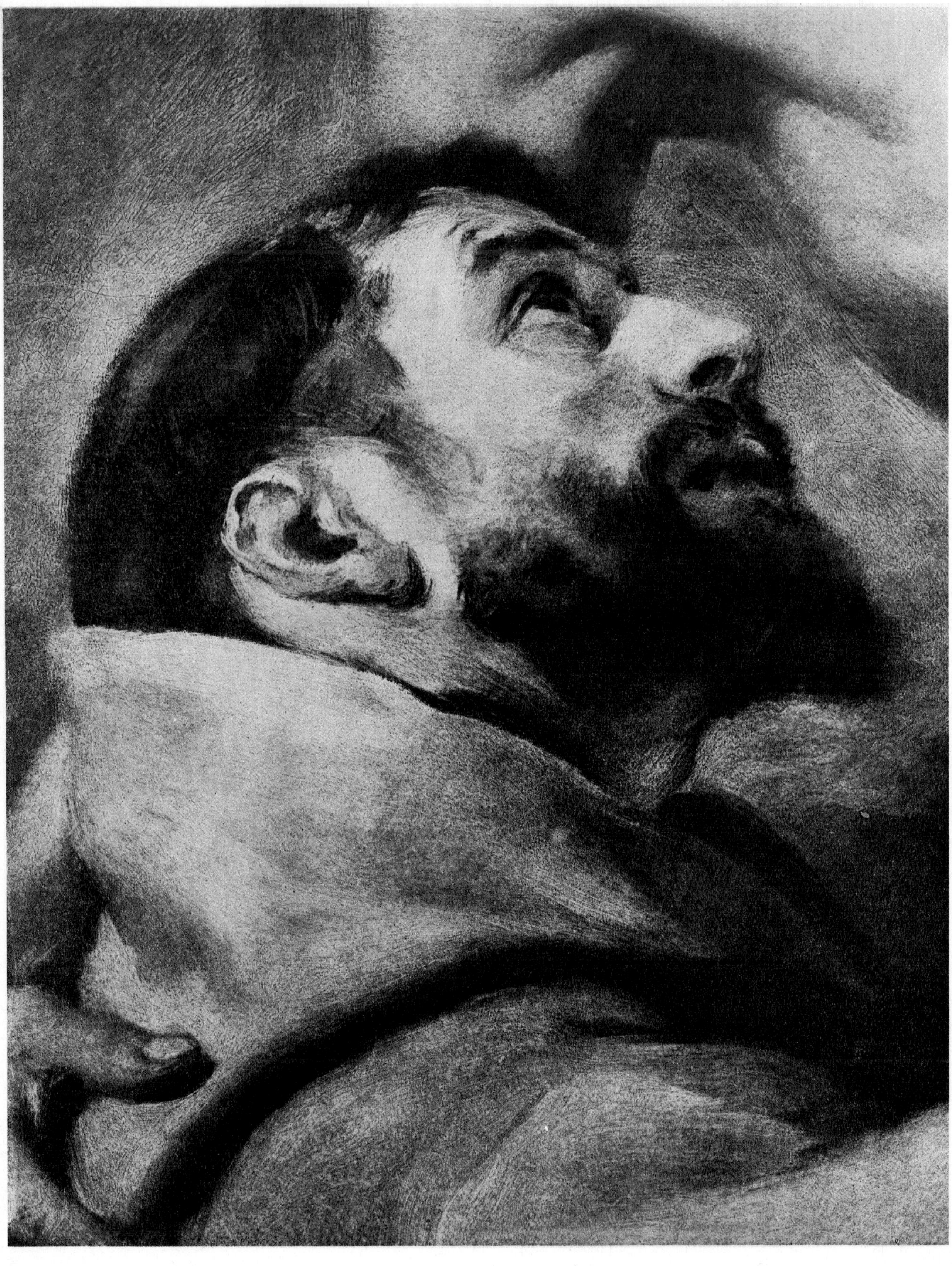

VI

BARTOLOMÉ ESTEBAN MURILLO

Boys eating Fruit. (Detail).
Circa 1650. — Canvas, 1,45 m. by 1,48 m.
Alte Pinakothek, Munich.

81

JUAN DE VALDÉS LEAL

The Temptation of St. Jerome.
1657 (signed and dated). — 2,22 m. by 2,47 m.
Provincial Museum, Seville. — Photo Arxiu Mas.

82

JUAN DE VALDÉS LEAL
The Flagellation of St. Jerome.
1657. — 2,22 m. by 2,47 m.
Provincial Museum, Seville. — Photo Arxiu Mas.

83

JUAN DE VALDÉS LEAL

« In ictu oculi ».
Circa 1671. — 2,20 m. by 2,16 m.
Church of the Hospital de la Caridad, Seville.
Photo Anderson.

IN ICTV OCVLI

84

CLAUDIO COELLO

Charles II adoring the Host (Detail).
1685-1688.
Monastery of the Escorial. — Photo Anderson.

REGALIS MENSA PRÆBEBIT DELICIAS REGIBUS

85

LUIS MELENDEZ
Self-Portrait.
1745 (signed and dated).
Musée du Louvre, Paris. — Photo Giraudon.

86

FRANCISCO BAYEU
Feliciana Bayeu, the Artist's Daughter.
0,38 m. by 0,30 m.
Prado, Madrid. — Photo Moreno.

87

MARIANO MAELLA

Charles IV.
1792 (signed and dated).
Museum, Mexico.

EL S.R D.N CARLOS IIII. REY DE ESPAÑA, Y EMPERADOR DE LAS YNDIAS, GEFE Y SOBERANO DE LA REAL Y DISTINGUIDA ORDEN ESPAÑOLA DE CARLOS III. SU AUGUSTO PADRE, Y
COMO GRAN MAESTRE DE ELLA, MANDO VARIAR EL MANTO DE LOS CABALLEROS EN LOS TERMINOS QUE DEMUESTRA ESTE RETRATO:
PROTECTOR BENEFICENTISSIMO DE ESTA REAL ACADEMIA DE S.N CARLOS DE NUEVA ESPAÑA, QUE FELIZMENTE REYNA.
AÑO DE 1792.

88

RAMON BAYEU

Promenade. — Tapestry cartoon.
2,60 m. by 1,42 m.
Spanish Embassy, London.

VII

FRANCISCO GOYA

Fernando Guillemardet.
Circa 1798. — Canvas, 1,85 m. by 1,25 m.
Musée du Louvre, Paris.

89

JOSÉ CASTILLO

The Flower Sellers. — Tapestry cartoon.
2,60 m. by 1,39 m.
Spanish Embassy, London.

FRANCISCO GOYA

The Flower Seller. — Tapestry cartoon.
1786. — 2,77 m. by 1,92 m.
Prado, Madrid. — Photo Ruiz Vernacci.

90

FRANCISCO GOYA

The Capture of Christ (Detail).
1788-1789.
Sacristy of the Cathedral of Toledo.
Photo Arxiu Mas.

91

FRANCISCO GOYA

Portrait of the actress María del Rosario Fernández. « La Tirana ».
1794 (signed and dated). — 1,12 m. by 0,79 m.
Private collection, Madrid. — Photo Moreno.

VIII

FRANCISCO GOYA

The Picnic.

1798. — Canvas, 0,41 m. by 0,26 m.

National Gallery, London.

92

FRANCISCO GOYA

The Pilgrimage to San Isidro (Detail).
Decoration for the dining-room of the « Quinta del Sordo »,
Goya's country house.
1,40 m. by 4,38 m.
Prado, Madrid. — Photo Anderson.

93

FRANCISCO GOYA

The 3rd of May 1808. Execution of the Defenders of Madrid.
Circa 1814. — 2,66 m. by 3,45 m.
Prado, Madrid. — Photo Ruiz Vernacci.

94

FRANCISCO GOYA

Portrait of Ferdinand VII.
1814 (signed). — 2,02 m. by 1,40 m.
Prado, Madrid. — Photo Anderson.

95

FRANCISCO GOYA

The Communion of St. José de Calasanz.
1819.
Church of the Escuelas Pîas de San Antón, Madrid.
Photo Moreno.

96

FRANCISCO GOYA

Head of a Monk.
Circa 1827. — 0,42 m. by 0,31 m.
Thomas Agnew and Sons, London.
Photo Cooper.

7938-1 ww

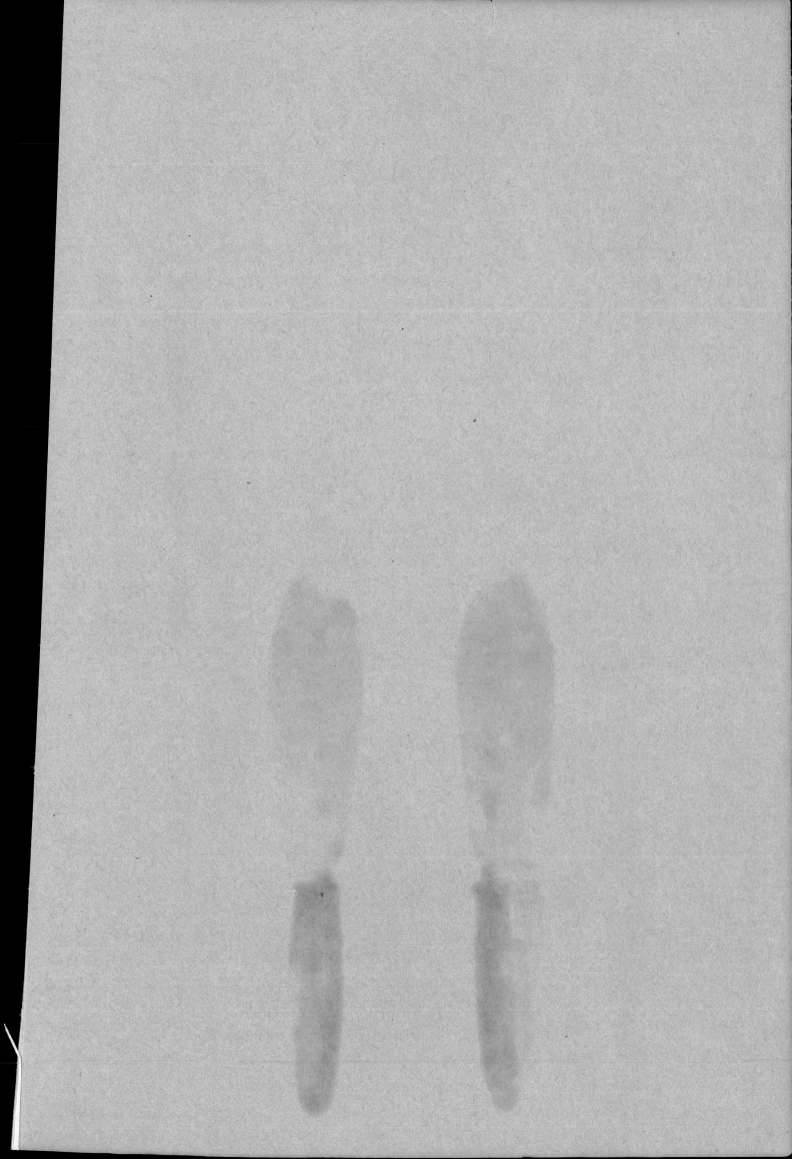

16798 OVERSIZE
ND
801
H3

HARRIS, E
SPANISH PAINTING

DATE DUE

GAYLORD PRINTED IN U.S.A.

F. J. B. & Co.
DEC. 1942
BINDERS